"Garfield's love of lasagna is well-documented. In his opinion, it's nature's perfect food. I'm often asked, 'Why lasagna?' Truth is, lasagna is MY favorite food. So, it looks like Garfield and I will be fighting over this delightful book."

—**Jim Davis,** creator of *Garfield*

"The sad truth is that lasagna—a dish of such great potential— is too often sloughed together haphazardly, a multithousand-calorie doorstop for the potluck table. Anna Hezel and the team from *TASTE* have, thankfully, reconsidered Garfield's favorite food and laid out, in friendly and encouraging words and pictures, simple and essential ways to elevate your lasagna game. Plus they've mapped out a great range of baked pastas and the lasagna-adjacent dishes of the world, so you can set sail from red sauce seas to faraway horizons, discovering variations of baked noodle bliss you may have never known were within your reach."

—**Peter Meehan,** food editor of the *Los Angeles Times* and cofounder of *Lucky Peach*

"An exuberant love letter to the bubbling, bronzed, bricklike comfort of lasagna. I foresee 200 percent more lasagna in my kitchen this fall, just as Anna Hezel and the editors of *TASTE* wanted for me."

—**Deb Perelman,** *Smitten Kitchen*

"Four of the greatest things to eat are tagliatelle Bolognese, spaghetti pomodoro, ricotta stuffed pasta, and pizza. Lasagna is all of that at once. This book shows the way and some wicked cool new stuff, too. Lasagna! If you don't like it, can we trust you?"

—**Brooks Headley,** chef and owner of Superiority Burger

Lasagna

Lasagna

A BAKED PASTA COOKBOOK

ANNA HEZEL AND THE EDITORS OF

TASTE

With recipes by Grace Parisi

Photographs by Dylan James Ho + Jeni Afuso

Clarkson Potter/Publishers

NEW YORK

CONTENTS

CHAPTER 1
THE CLASSICS 26

CHAPTER 2
NOT CLASSICS 46

WHY LASAGNA?

In 1970, on her television show The French Chef, Julia Child made lasagna. In the famous episode (which still exists in various corners of the Internet), she accidentally skips the garlic, forgets what ricotta cheese is called, and invents colorful terms like "spaghetti laundry" and "inner sauce" on the spot. Through it all, she makes one thing clear: Lasagna is a novel, new concept to her.

Half a century later, the layered pasta dish is so embedded in the American zeitgeist that it finds itself the subject of Kylie Jenner Snapchats, Chrissy Teigen Instagram Stories, and countless memes. America continues to cook lasagna, and to seek inspiration from chefs and TV personalities including Giada De Laurentiis, Ree Drummond, Michael Solomonov, and Marcus Samuelsson. We turn leftover braises and sauces into late-night baked-pasta masterpieces and spend rainy Sundays simmering ragus and cranking out thin, velvety layers of fresh pasta. In today's age, it's absurd–though also a little endearing–to imagine that a famous TV chef like Julia wouldn't know her way around a lasagna.

Maybe we should thank Marcella Hazan, the Julia Child of Italian cooking, for writing so many seminal cookbooks devoted to the fundamentals of the cuisine. Or perhaps we owe it to the ever-multiplying Olive Gardens that punctuate suburban neighborhoods throughout the country for bringing a whole pantry of Italian ingredients and dishes into the American lexicon. Or maybe credit goes to Garfield, who's been dutifully eating meaty two-dimensional cubes of it in newspaper comics and on television screens since 1978. What we can say without hesitation is that lasagna is here, and it's here to stay.

Lasagna is such a part of the collective consciousness that it has become cultural shorthand for comfort. It's not uncommon to take a foil-wrapped Pyrex dish of lasagna to welcome a new baby home from the hospital. In the dead of winter, we make reassuring batches on cold nights to conjure strength to greet the week ahead. We stockpile it in our freezers as a safeguard against the unexpected (or simply to look forward to).

Lasagna may be imprinted in our minds as a dish made by *nonnas* or served against a background of red checkered tablecloths, but its history is more complicated than simply sprouting up from some bucolic, cypress-dappled town in Italy. The dish we know today could not exist without the egg-and-wheat pasta dough that was allegedly introduced into the cuisine by the ancient Greeks, or the tomatoes that explorers took to Italy from Central America in the sixteenth century.

There are theories that the name "lasagna" comes from the ancient Greek word *laganon*, meaning a dough that is cut into strips (essentially flat, wide pasta). It could also be named for the ancient Roman pot that the layered pasta was baked in, called a *lasana*. The first written recipe for a baked dish with alternating layers of meat and dough came from a book called *De re coquinaria* that was attributed to a Roman gourmet named Apicius in the first century A.D. The recipe (which contains no pasta, tomatoes, or cheese) describes a stew made from fish and sow's udder and instructs you to "prepare layers of stew and pancakes, interspersed with oil" before baking it all in a metal dish.

In this book, we're going to spare you the sow's udder and skip ahead a few centuries to the good stuff–like layers of meat sauce and ricotta cheese, buttery béchamels, and

Bolognese ragus that you might eat if you were invited to dinner anywhere from Emilia-Romagna to Erie, Pennsylvania. We'll look at some of the dish's Greek counterparts and precursors (like moussaka and pastitsio), and we'll see how Italian colonialism on the Horn of Africa culminated in a rebelliously peppery berbere-spiked lasagna topped with bright orange Cheddar cheese.

And because this is a cookbook of very good pasta, cheese, and sauce combinations, we'll dive into the wide world of baked pastas as well, from shells that are plumped up with ricotta, to a wildly cheesy, maximalist take on mac and cheese. The noodles might not be wide and flat, but these are pastas that channel the same warmth and spirit as lasagna–dishes you'll want to gather, drink, and laugh around.

We want to think of lasagna not just as a set of grandma's recipes that is frozen in time and space, but as a dish that continues to evolve, warp, bubble up, and melt as it sails around the globe and passes from generation to generation. Let this book be your license to make yourself a personal skillet of spaghetti pie or ravioli lasagna after a tough day of work, to skip the cheese and the tomato sauce altogether like Apicius did, or to turn your favorite Italian sub or porchetta sandwich into a lasagna. Why? Because you can.

— **Anna Hezel, TASTE**

THE ANATOMY OF LASAGNA

We each have an archetypal lasagna.

Maybe it's the one from the Stouffer's commercials, or perhaps the one your family used to go out for on special trips to your town's Little Italy. In this book, along with the classics, you'll find new interpretations that will challenge that archetype and stretch the definition of lasagna to the wildest, farthest possibilities of what it can be–whether that means it's bright pink thanks to grated beets, packed with heat from an Ethiopian berbere spice blend, or turned

into dessert with Nutella and marshmallows. Will it always require wide, flat noodles? Most of the time. Does it have to have cheese? Not always! Is meat required? No way.

More than a static list of ingredients, lasagna is all about the architecturte and the ways that cheeses, vegetable purees, and meat braises can hoist up layers, creating just enough room between the pasta barriers to collect stray bits of tart tomato sauces and creamy béchamels. The individual components (which we'll get to in the next few pages) are important, but assembly is its own fun little engineering project. Here's our blueprint for the ultimate lasagna construction.

The Toasty Top:

A great bubbly, brown lasagna hinges on a good layer of cheese on top. When you've laid down your final pasta layer, you should still have about a cup left of shredded cheese (or béchamel) to cover the top. In the case of the Beet-Ricotta Lasagna with Brown Butter & Poppy Seeds (page 54), we'll show you how to create a golden topping from brown butter. In A Potentially Vegan Puttanesca Lasagna (page 50), we'll show you how to do it with a little bit of sauce and extra olive oil.

The Fillings:

Start out with any spreadable fillings you have, like ricotta cheese, tomato sauce, or purees. If there's a layer of roasted vegetables, leafy greens, or meat, scatter this across the sauce layer. Once that's in place, give the layer a little sprinkle of cheese (if cheese is called for).

The Pasta:

Next, lay down your noodles in parallel rows. The noodles will expand in the oven as they absorb liquid, so they ideally overlap only slightly.

The Bottom Sauce:

At the bottom of the pan, before you begin construction, it's a good idea to start with a ladleful of sauce spread across the pan's surface to prevent the pasta from turning into starchy concrete in the oven.

PICK YOUR PASTA

There are lasagnas that benefit from eggy, paper-thin Fresh Pasta Sheets (page 129), but there are also times when you crave the slightly burnt, slightly crunchy edges of a classic, curly lasagna noodle from a box. And let's face it: There are also times when you're so hungry that you're willing to use whatever type of noodle you see first on the grocery store shelf. Here are a few pasta options and things to keep in mind when using each.

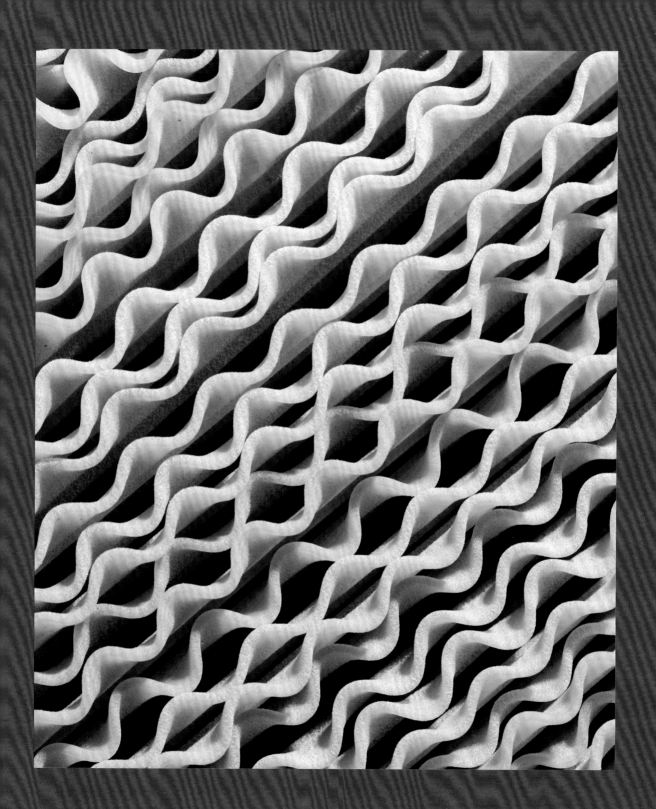

DRY LASAGNA NOODLES

They're available at every grocery store. They're easy to use. They often have the trademark curly edges that hold on tightly to ragus and get brown and crunchy in the oven. Just follow the instructions on the package–generally you boil the noodles for 8 minutes, lay them out on a lightly greased baking sheet (or piece of plastic wrap) so they don't all stick together, and you're ready to assemble your lasagna. Chances are, a few will break or stick together, but each box usually has enough to account for some minor casualties.

An important thing to keep in mind is that the cooked noodles tend to keep absorbing moisture, even after the lasagna has come out of the oven, so if you're using a thin sauce, the noodles can potentially get a little bit mushy. For that reason, boxed noodles are best for chunky, meaty sauces or lasagnas with fillings that err on the dry side.

HOW TO COOK DRY LASAGNA NOODLES

Bring a large pot of salted water to a boil. Add the lasagna noodles and cook, stirring occasionally, according to the package directions, until al dente. Drain and rinse under cold water. Arrange the noodles on a lightly greased baking sheet or a piece of plastic wrap and use as instructed.

NO-BOIL LASAGNA NOODLES

These are also available at many grocery stores and are generally labeled "no boil" or "oven ready." Although some people flinch at the idea of "instant" ingredients, no-cook lasagna noodles are actually regular old noodles that have been precooked and then dehydrated. When you layer them with something saucy and put them in the oven, they'll cook all the way through very easily.

On top of the convenience, no-cook noodles tend to be thinner than classic dry noodles, so you can get a little closer to the texture and thickness of fresh pasta without actually cranking any dough through the finest setting on your pasta machine. Since they only cook when they come in contact with sauce or liquid, you just have to be a little bit fastidious about covering every inch as you assemble your lasagna.

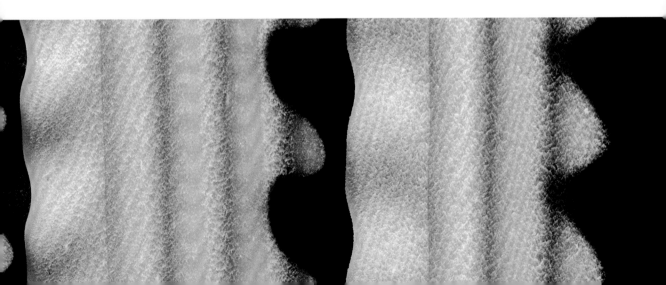

HOMEMADE FRESH PASTA

With all of these options a mere grocery store trip away, why would you make your own pasta from scratch? (Besides the obvious advantage of pretending to be an Italian grandmother–or grandfather–and kneading and rolling dough until it's smooth and elastic while belting out amateur Puccini?)

From a practical standpoint, the great thing about making your own pasta dough is that you can make it as thin or thick as you want, and you only have to precook it for about a minute before layering it into the baking dish. The gentle, chewy bite and fresh, mildly eggy flavor are great in lasagnas like the Carbonara Lasagna on page 49.

WONTON WRAPPERS

You heard us. Wonton wrappers, which are usually sold frozen or stacked near the refrigerated tofu section of most large grocery stores, are made from the same ingredients that most store-bought pastas are–that is, essentially, flour and water. They're usually vegan, they don't need to be cooked before using, and they keep their soft, paper-thin, slightly elastic structure even after baking. The one major pitfall of wonton wrappers is that they are coated with a layer of cornstarch to prevent them from sticking together. Starch absorbs moisture, so if you're using wonton wrappers for layers, stick to saucy lasagnas that have liquid to spare (like the Classic Bolognese & Béchamel Lasagna on page 42 or the Classic Meat Sauce & Ricotta Lasagna on page 28.

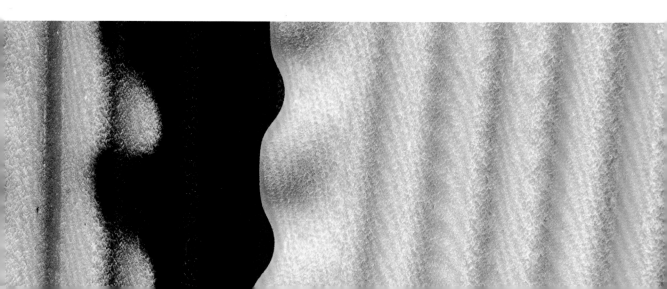

PICK YOUR SAUCE

One of the most enjoyable things about contemplating a lasagna strategy is that you can transform almost anything into a tray of the stuff. Leftover Sunday gravy? Tomato sauce and meatballs from your spaghetti dinner the other night? An aromatic lamb, braised in wine? Rotisserie chicken? All can become lasagna with a little bit of shrewd cheese-and-pasta planning. Since the pasta in a lasagna is usually boiled briefly first, then finishes cooking in the oven, picking a sauce is all about finding the right balance of moisture so that your lasagna doesn't dry out or get too soggy.

CLASSIC & SIMPLE RED SAUCE

A good basic tomato sauce is like that pair of jeans you own that you've worn to meetings, to cocktail parties, and to groggily walk your dog at dawn: It's flexible and reliable, and it pulls everything together. Our recipe on page 130 works with many of the recipes in this book; the texture and thickness is designed so that a little bit of the moisture will be absorbed into the pasta in the oven, and you'll be left with a lasagna that's saucy but not damp.

MEAT SAUCES

In lasagnas made with meat sauces, chunky ragus, and braises, the sauces have the starring roles (think of them as your protein protagonists). Some of our favorites are the Red Wine–Braised Short Rib Lasagna (page 68), the Moroccan-Spiced Lamb Lasagna (page 77), the Lasagna with Meatballs & Sunday Sauce (page 31), and the Classic Bolognese & Béchamel Lasagna (page 42).

VEGETABLE PUREES

In addition to adding texture to a sauce or even between the layers, you can also use vegetables as the creamy or saucy element in lasagna. In the Accidentally Vegan Sweet Corn & Scallion Lasagna (page 57), we decided to skip the ricotta cheese altogether in favor of a creamy corn puree.

PESTO

When it comes to pesto, there are two important things to keep in mind. First, a little goes a long way with this potent blend of raw garlic and fresh herbs. Secondly, the only moisture comes from the olive oil, so it's not a particularly wet sauce. This means that if you're incorporating pesto into a lasagna, it shouldn't be your only source of moisture. One way to work around this is to stir it into the ricotta cheese (like we show you on page 136), or layer it with the cheese (like we do in the Lasagna with Kale Pesto on page 52).

PICK YOUR CHEESE

Like the chorus in a Greek comedy, cheese serves a lot of functions in lasagna. In the case of ricotta, it can be the snow-white barrier between the pasta and the sauce. Cheese can also be added to béchamel, essentially turning it into a Mornay sauce. And who could forgo the golden-brown and bubbling molten cheese icing on this noodle cake? There are lots of different cheese options when it comes to lasagna. Here are some of our favorites.

SOFT CHEESES

Ricotta's mildness and soft, ever-so-slightly fluffy texture make it the ideal buffer between pasta and sauce. It has enough firmness to give the layers a little bit of height, and it absorbs flavor and color from the sauce. Some Italian-American recipes from the 1980s and '90s that predated the wide availability of ricotta called for cottage cheese instead. This may sound a little blasphemous, but moms in the Midwest have been swearing by it for decades, and plenty of people claim it's a dead ringer for ricotta once it's all been baked together.

Cream cheese? Yes, we endorse this move, though sparingly. It comes in handy when you're looking for a denser texture and a little more acidity. In our Spinach Artichoke Dip Lasagna (page 76), the cream cheese melts into the vegetables to create a rich filling that can stand on its own without any sauce. In our Sweet Crespelle with Lemon & Tart Cherry Sauce (page 116), cream cheese forms the base of a sweet filling for a fruity dessert version of the tomato-covered manicotti we know and love.

HARD CHEESES

When you see Parmesan or Pecorino Romano in a recipe, it's most likely there to contribute flavor rather than texture or structure. These are intensely salty aged cheeses that have very low moisture content, so they're often grated and added to something that does have a lot of moisture, like a béchamel or a ricotta. These types of cheeses have a higher melting point than their softer counterparts, so when we ask you to finely grate some and sprinkle it on top of a lasagna in this book, it's less about creating a melty top and more about adding another layer of flavor—just like you might sprinkle a little bit of flaky salt onto a finished dish.

MELTY CHEESES

When it comes to getting that perfect slow-motion cheese pull when you lift out the first square of lasagna from a hot pan (you know—the one you've seen on Instagram Stories or in Stouffer's commercials), you're going to need a cheese that's designed for melting. In the Classic Meat Sauce & Ricotta Lasagna (page 28), mozzarella does the heavy lifting. In the Ethiopian Lasagna (page 35), it's all about the melty orange Cheddar. There are a lot of options in the universe of lasagna cheese, but the ones you'll see most often in this book are Taleggio, Fontina, mozzarella, and Monterey Jack.

THE CLASSICS

Say you wake up tomorrow morning to a polite knock on your door from a group of E.T.-looking alien fools, demanding the answer to one simple question about humanity: What is lasagna? Armed with this chapter, you could provide a pretty well-rounded answer.

In these first eight recipes, you'll find the most foundational formulas of pasta, sauce, and cheese. There are lasagnas you'll recognize from your grandma's kitchen, the ice-crusted box of Stouffer's in the back of your freezer, or the charmingly dysfunctional red-sauce joint in your neighborhood.

Later in the book, we'll dig deeper into the world of baked pastas like elegant lasagna timpanos and new interpretations like crunchy life-changing deep-fried bricks of lasagna. But for now, let's start with the classics.

CLASSIC MEAT SAUCE & RICOTTA LASAGNA

8 TO 12 SERVINGS

This is the most essential, cartooniest lasagna in this book–definitely *Garfield*-approved. When they create a lasagna emoji (fingers crossed!), this will be the model: wavy noodles, fluffy ricotta, a sweet tomato sauce full of ground beef, and a lightly blistered layer of gooey mozzarella crowning the top. Classic and simple, this is the lasagna you'll dig into over warm, raucous gatherings full of mismatched plates and spilled Chianti.

Meat Sauce

2 tablespoons extra-virgin olive oil

1 small yellow onion, finely chopped

2 large garlic cloves, minced

12 ounces (¾ pound) extra-lean ground beef (96% lean)

4 tablespoons tomato paste

1 (28-ounce) can tomato puree

1 teaspoon sugar

½ teaspoon dried oregano, crumbled

½ teaspoon dried thyme

1 dried bay leaf

Coarse kosher salt (preferably Diamond Crystal) and freshly ground black pepper

Lasagna

2 pounds ricotta cheese

2 tablespoons finely chopped flat-leaf parsley

2 ounces freshly grated Parmesan cheese (about ½ cup)

1 pound low-moisture mozzarella cheese (not fresh), shredded (about 4 cups)

2 teaspoons coarse kosher salt (preferably Diamond Crystal)

¼ teaspoon freshly ground black pepper

1 large egg, beaten

15 dry lasagna noodles, cooked and cooled (see page 16)

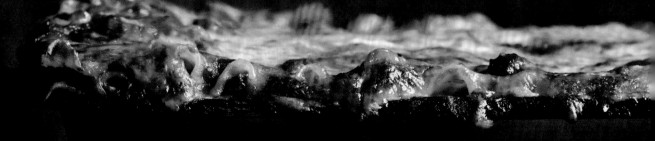

1. Make the meat sauce: Heat the olive oil in a medium pot over medium heat until shimmering, about 2 minutes. Add the onion and garlic and cook over medium-high heat, stirring occasionally, until lightly browned, 5 to 6 minutes. Add the ground beef and cook, breaking up the meat with a wooden spoon, until just beginning to brown, about 10 minutes. Add the tomato paste and cook, stirring gently, until the paste darkens slightly, 1 to 2 minutes. Add the tomato puree, sugar, oregano, thyme, bay leaf, and 3 cups water. Season with 1 teaspoon salt and ¼ teaspoon pepper and bring to a boil. Cover partially, reduce the heat to low, and simmer until the sauce is thick and has reduced to about 6 cups, about 45 minutes. Season to taste with salt and pepper. Reserve 4 cups of the sauce for the lasagna and keep the rest warm for serving. Discard the bay leaf.

2. Make the cheese mixture: Preheat the oven to 375°F and position a rack in the center. In a large bowl, combine the ricotta, parsley, ¼ cup of the Parmesan, two thirds (about 2⅔ cups) of the mozzarella (reserve the remaining cheese for the top), the salt, and the pepper. Add the egg and stir to combine.

3. Assemble the lasagna: Spread 1 cup of the meat sauce in the bottom of a 9 x 13-inch (3-quart) glass or ceramic baking dish. Arrange 5 of the noodles, overlapping slightly, in the dish. Spoon half of the ricotta mixture onto the noodles, then use the back of the spoon or a butter knife to spread in an even layer. Top with 1 cup of the sauce, spreading evenly. Arrange another 5 noodles on top, followed by the remaining ricotta mixture and another 1 cup sauce. Arrange the remaining noodles on top and spread with an even layer of 1 cup sauce.

4. Bake the lasagna: Sprinkle the remaining mozzarella and Parmesan on top and bake until the top is browned, the noodles are crusty around the edges, and the sauce is bubbling, about 45 minutes. Remove the lasagna from the oven and set it aside to rest for 20 minutes before cutting into squares and serving. Serve the remaining sauce on the side.

LASAGNA WITH MEATBALLS & SUNDAY SAUCE

If you manage to make a batch of Sunday Sauce (page 134), there is a definite chance that you will accidentally keep wandering into the kitchen in a sausage-scented daze, taking a taste here and there until the whole pot has somehow vanished. If your sauce survives its two-hour simmer, however, then you're going to want to make a pan of this lasagna. The sauce is meaty enough (from a combination of Italian sausage, meatballs, and pork shoulder) that it feels less like a sauce and more like a hearty, spicy three-course meal hiding under sheets of curly noodles and golden-brown Pecorino Romano cheese.

10 TO 12 SERVINGS

2 pounds ricotta cheese

¼ cup finely chopped flat-leaf parsley

2 tablespoons finely chopped fresh basil leaves

2 ounces Pecorino Romano cheese, freshly grated (about ½ cup)

1 pound low-moisture mozzarella cheese (not fresh), shredded (about 4 cups)

2 teaspoons coarse kosher salt (preferably Diamond Crystal)

¼ teaspoon freshly ground black pepper

2 large eggs, beaten

½ recipe Sunday Sauce (page 134), meat and sauce separated (12 meatballs, 4 cups sauce, 2 sausages, and half of the braised pork), warm

15 dry lasagna noodles, cooked and cooled (see page 16)

1. ***Make the cheese mixture:*** Preheat the oven to 375°F and position a rack in the center. In a large bowl, combine the ricotta, parsley, and basil. Add ¼ cup of the Pecorino Romano cheese and 2⅔ cups of the mozzarella (reserve the remaining cheese for the top) and season with the salt and pepper. Add the eggs and stir to combine.

2. ***Assemble the lasagna:*** Cut the 12 meatballs from the Sunday Sauce in half. Spread 1 cup of the sauce (no meat) in the bottom of a 9 x 13-inch (3-quart) glass or ceramic baking dish. Arrange 5 of the noodles, overlapping slightly, in the dish. Spoon half of the ricotta mixture onto the noodles,

spreading to an even layer. Top with 1 cup of the sauce and half of the meatballs, sausages, and pork. Arrange another 5 noodles on top, followed by the remaining ricotta mixture, 1 cup sauce, and the remaining 6 meatballs, 1 sausage, and the pork. Arrange the remaining 5 noodles on top and spread with the remaining 1 cup sauce. In a small bowl, toss together the remaining mozzarella and Pecorino Romano and sprinkle over the lasagna.

3. ***Bake the lasagna:*** Bake until the top is browned and crusty around the edges and bubbling, about 45 minutes. Let the lasagna rest for 20 minutes before cutting into squares and serving.

CREAMY MUSHROOM LASAGNA

This simplified lasagna is built around a few handfuls of mushrooms that require only about fifteen minutes to caramelize on the stovetop. Since mushrooms are the star here, it's a great opportunity to use those blue oysters you found at the co-op, or the chestnut mushrooms you picked up at the greenmarket. If you end up sticking to the standard creminis and oysters from the grocery store, rest assured the final result will still taste great.

Lasagna

2 pounds mushrooms, cleaned and sliced (oyster, cremini, and chanterelle varieties are all great)

1 large shallot, halved and thinly sliced (about ¾ cup)

1½ teaspoons chopped fresh rosemary

1½ teaspoons chopped fresh sage

1½ teaspoons chopped fresh thyme

3 tablespoons unsalted butter

¼ cup extra-virgin olive oil

Coarse kosher salt (preferably Diamond Crystal) and freshly ground black pepper

2 pounds ricotta cheese (4 cups)

2 ounces Parmesan cheese, freshly grated (about ½ cup)

1 pound Fontina cheese, coarsely grated

15 dry lasagna noodles, cooked and cooled (see page 16)

Béchamel

3 tablespoons unsalted butter

¼ cup all-purpose flour

3 cups whole milk

Pinch of freshly grated nutmeg

Coarse kosher salt and freshly ground black pepper

1. Cook the mushrooms: Preheat the oven to 375°F and position the oven rack in the center. In a large bowl, combine the mushrooms, shallot, and herbs. In a very large skillet set over medium heat, melt 3 tablespoons of the butter with the olive oil. Add the mushroom mixture and cook over moderately high heat, stirring occasionally, until the liquid is evaporated and the mushrooms are golden, about 12 minutes. Season with ½ teaspoon salt and a pinch of pepper, and transfer to a bowl. Set aside.

2. Make the cheese mixtures: In a medium bowl, combine the ricotta with half of the Parmesan and season with ½ teaspoon salt and ¼ teaspoon pepper. In another bowl, combine the Fontina and remaining Parmesan.

(recipe continues)

3. Make the béchamel: In a medium saucepan, melt the remaining 3 tablespoons of butter over medium heat. Whisk in the flour and cook over moderately high heat, whisking constantly (be sure to get into the edges of the pan—a flat whisk works best), until lightly golden and fragrant, about 3 minutes. Whisk in the milk all at once and bring to a boil. Reduce the heat to very low, and whisk until the sauce is thick, about 8 minutes. Add the nutmeg and season with 1 teaspoon salt and ¼ teaspoon pepper.

4. Assemble the lasagna: Spread a thin layer of béchamel (about ½ cup) on the bottom of a 9 x 13-inch (3-quart) glass or ceramic baking dish. Arrange 5 of the noodles, slightly overlapping, in the dish. Add half of the ricotta mixture, spreading it to an even layer, and top with half of the mushrooms. Top with one third of the Fontina mixture. Drizzle with one third of the remaining béchamel sauce. Repeat with 5 more noodles, the remaining ricotta and mushrooms, half of the remaining Fontina mixture, and half of the remaining béchamel. Top with the remaining 5 noodles, Fontina mixture, and béchamel.

5. Bake the lasagna: Cover the baking dish loosely with foil and bake for 30 minutes. Uncover and bake until golden and bubbling, 20 to 25 minutes longer. Let rest for 15 minutes before cutting into squares and serving.

ETHIOPIAN LASAGNA

For Hannah Giorgis, a journalist and *TASTE* contributor, Ethiopia and Eritrea are as much a part of lasagna's history as Italy or the United States. As a result of Italy's long, complicated past as a colonizer of these countries in the Horn of Africa, lasagna has found its way onto party buffets right alongside the *injera* and the *doro wat*. In Hannah's recipe, green onions, berbere (a spice mix of ginger, chiles, nigella, and fenugreek), and smoky paprika scent the meat sauce, and the whole thing is topped with a sprinkling of mozzarella and orange Cheddar cheese to give it a warm, golden hue.

Meat Sauce

¼ cup extra-virgin olive oil

1 large yellow onion, diced

2 large fresh tomatoes, chopped

2 scallions, white and green parts, thinly sliced

8 large garlic cloves, minced

1½ pounds ground beef (85% lean)

1 teaspoon coarse kosher salt (preferably Diamond Crystal), plus more to taste

¼ teaspoon freshly ground black pepper, plus more to taste

1 tablespoon tomato paste

1 tablespoon berbere spice mix (or more to taste)

2 (15-ounce) cans tomato sauce

2 dried bay leaves

1 tablespoon smoked paprika

1 tablespoon ground coriander

1 tablespoon dried oregano

2 tablespoons chopped fresh basil leaves

Lasagna

Olive oil or softened butter for baking dish

1 pound mozzarella cheese, shredded (about 4 cups)

8 ounces orange Cheddar cheese, shredded (about 2 cups)

15 dry lasagna noodles, cooked and cooled (see page 16)

2 ounces freshly grated Parmesan cheese (about ½ cup)

Pan spray

1. Make the meat sauce: Heat the olive oil in a large heavy-bottomed pot or Dutch oven over medium heat. Add the onion and cook gently without browning until soft, about 3 minutes, then stir in the tomatoes, scallions, and garlic. Cook until the tomatoes are broken down and the liquid is slightly reduced, 3 to 5 minutes.

(recipe continues)

2. Add the beef to the pot, breaking up clumps with a wooden spoon. Add the salt and pepper, then cook until the meat is browned, about 15 minutes. If you prefer a thinner sauce, add about ½ cup water to the meat as it cooks.

3. Stir in the tomato paste and berbere and cook until slightly darkened and fragrant, 2 to 3 minutes, before adding the tomato sauce, bay leaves, paprika, coriander, oregano, and basil. Reduce the heat and simmer, stirring occasionally, until the sauce is thickened and slightly reduced, about 20 minutes. Season to taste with salt and pepper. Discard the bay leaves.

4. Preheat the oven to 375°F with the rack in the center and grease a 9 x 13-inch (3-quart) glass or ceramic baking dish with olive oil or softened butter.

5. **Make the cheese mixture:** Just before you are ready to assemble the lasagna, stir 1 cup of the mozzarella directly into the sauce. In a bowl, combine the remaining 3 cups of mozzarella with the Cheddar.

6. **Assemble the lasagna:** Ladle ½ cup of the meat sauce mixture into the baking dish, spreading to cover evenly. Follow with a layer of 5 noodles, then one third of the remaining sauce, then one third of the mixed cheeses. repeat with 5 more noodles, half of the remaining sauce, and half of the remaining mixed cheeses. Top with the remaining 5 noodles, sauce, and mixed cheeses. Sprinkle the Parmesan over the top layer of mozzarella and Cheddar.

7. **Bake the lasagna:** Spray the shiny side of a sheet of aluminum foil with pan spray, then cover the lasagna with the greased side facing down, folding the edges over the sides of the pan. Bake covered for 45 minutes, then remove the foil and bake for another 15 minutes or until a significant portion of the top cheese layer has browned. Allow to cool for at least 30 minutes before slicing and serving.

SUMMER VEGGIE LASAGNA

Do you ever think back wistfully to the 1990s and wonder why we stopped putting zucchini, bell peppers, and button mushrooms in everything? This recipe resurrects the Clinton-era combination in baked-pasta form. By seasoning and browning all of the vegetables together before layering them in the pasta, you draw out the moisture and caramelize and intensify their sweetness so your veggies are extra flavorful. Adding a bit of fresh parsley and crushed fennel seeds (hallmark seasonings of a good sweet Italian sausage) keeps the flavors bright and fresh.

2 tablespoons extra-virgin olive oil

8 ounces white button mushrooms, stemmed and quartered

1 small yellow onion, cut into ½-inch pieces

Coarse kosher salt (preferably Diamond Crystal) and freshly ground black pepper

1 pound red bell peppers, cored, seeded, and cut into ½-inch pieces

1 pound zucchini, trimmed and cut into ½-inch pieces

½ teaspoon crushed fennel seeds or fennel pollen

1 pound ricotta cheese

2 tablespoons chopped flat-leaf parsley

2 ounces freshly grated Parmesan cheese (about ½ cup)

1 large egg

8 ounces low-moisture mozzarella cheese (not fresh), shredded

1 recipe (4½ cups) Classic & Simple Red Sauce (page 130), warm

15 dry lasagna noodles, cooked and cooled (see page 16)

1. Cook the vegetables: Preheat the oven to 375°F and position a rack in the center. Heat 1 tablespoon of the oil in a large skillet over medium-high heat until shimmering. Add the mushrooms and cook, stirring occasionally, until any liquid is evaporated and the mushrooms are lightly browned, 8 to 12 minutes. Add the onion, season with 1 teaspoon salt and ¼ teaspoon black pepper, and cook, stirring occasionally, until the onion is translucent, about 5 minutes. Add the remaining oil and the bell peppers, zucchini, and fennel seeds or pollen and cook, stirring occasionally, until the vegetables are lightly browned and tender, about 10 minutes longer. Season generously with salt and pepper.

2. Make the cheese mixture: In a medium bowl, combine the ricotta, parsley, and half of the Parmesan and season to taste with ½ teaspoon salt and ¼ teaspoon pepper. Stir in the egg and half of the mozzarella.

3. Assemble the lasagna: Spread ½ cup of the red sauce in the bottom of a 9 x 13-inch (3-quart) glass or ceramic baking dish. Arrange 5 of the noodles, overlapping slightly, in the dish. Spoon half of the ricotta mixture onto the noodles, spreading to an even layer, followed by half of the vegetables. Top with 1½ cups of the sauce. Arrange another 5 noodles on top, followed by the remaining ricotta mixture and vegetables and another 1½ cups sauce. Arrange the remaining noodles on top and spread with the remaining sauce.

4. Bake the lasagna: Sprinkle the remaining mozzarella and Parmesan on top and bake until the top is browned and crusty around the edges and the cheese is bubbling, about 45 minutes. Let the lasagna rest 20 minutes before cutting into squares and serving.

SLOW-COOKER SPINACH RICOTTA LASAGNA

A slow-cooker lasagna recipe? Believe. Since the countertop crock traps in moisture and maintains a consistent low temperature, you can construct this lasagna with totally uncooked pasta (yes, really). All the ingredients (the baby spinach, the ricotta, the red sauce) hang out and cook together for three and a half hours, and come dinnertime, the noodles have absorbed any extra liquid, and the basil and spinach have played nicely with the cheeses. Is your slow cooker round? Or oval shaped? No problem–just break the pasta up into slightly smaller pieces as you go so it all fits.

2 tablespoons extra-virgin olive oil

1 small yellow onion, chopped

2 large garlic cloves, minced

1 teaspoon finely chopped fresh rosemary

¼ teaspoon dried red pepper flakes

10 ounces baby spinach

Coarse kosher salt (preferably Diamond Crystal) and freshly ground black pepper

2 cups (15 ounces) ricotta cheese

3 tablespoons chopped fresh basil leaves

1 pound low-moisture mozzarella cheese (not fresh), shredded (about 4 cups)

1 recipe (4½ cups) Classic & Simple Red Sauce (page 130), warm

9 dry, curly lasagna noodles (uncooked)

1. **Make the spinach-and-cheese mixture:** Set a 5-quart slow cooker to the high heat setting and preheat while you prepare the filling. Heat the olive oil in a large skillet over medium heat. Add the onion and cook on high heat, stirring occasionally, until lightly browned, about 5 minutes. Add the garlic, rosemary, and red pepper flakes and cook until fragrant, about 1 minute. Add the spinach to the skillet in large handfuls and give it a few stirs, allowing each handful to wilt for about a minute before adding more. Season to taste with salt and black pepper and transfer to a colander to drain and cool slightly. Gently press the spinach to extract some of the liquid.

2. In a bowl, combine the ricotta, basil, three fourths of the mozzarella (about 3 cups; save the remaining mozzarella for the top), ½ teaspoon salt, and ½ teaspoon black pepper. Fold in the spinach.

Assemble the lasagna: Spoon 1 cup of the sauce into the slow cooker. Arrange 3 lasagna noodles over the sauce, breaking them to fit and cover any empty spots. Spread half of the ricotta mixture over the noodles and top with 1 cup of the sauce. Top with 3 more noodles, breaking to fit. Add the remaining ricotta mixture and another cup of the sauce. Top with the remaining 3 noodles, breaking to fit, and the remaining sauce. ●

3. Slow cook the lasagna: Cover the slow cooker, placing a clean kitchen towel between the lid and the slow cooker to catch condensation. Cook on high heat until the noodles are tender and the sauce is absorbed, about 3½ hours. Sprinkle the remaining mozzarella on top, cover, and cook until melted, about 10 minutes. Turn cooker off and let rest, uncovered, for 15 minutes before cutting into squares and serving.

To Make In the Oven

Use 15 cooked noodles (5 for each layer; see page 16), and assemble in a 9 x 13-inch (3-quart) glass or ceramic baking dish according to the instructions opposite. Top with mozzarella and bake, uncovered, at 375°F for 45 minutes. Let rest for 15 minutes before serving.

CLASSIC BOLOGNESE & BÉCHAMEL LASAGNA

There are times when you want a lasagna packed with melty, stretchy cheese. This is not that time; lasagna Bolognese is for when you want to spotlight subtle flavors and textures like peppery nutmeg in a Parmesan-laced béchamel with butter-softened celery and carrots in the rich, beefy ragu. Lasagna Bolognese takes time to make (the sauce alone takes about ninety minutes), but the payoff is enormous. If you're having people over for Sunday dinner, or just trying to get your family to sit down at the same time for a shared meal, make the sauce a day or two before, and make lots of it (the recipe doubles easily) for a quicker overall prep time. By the way, Bolognese sauce gets better overnight in the refrigerator (and is pure gold when you find some hidden in the freezer), and, bonus, you can use leftovers as a spaghetti topping all week long.

Unsalted butter, for the dish

1 recipe (4 cups) Thick Béchamel (page 139)

½ recipe (6 sheets; about 8 ounces) Fresh Pasta Sheets (page 129)

½ recipe (3 cups) Ragu Bolognese (page 133), warm

4 ounces freshly grated Parmesan cheese (about 1 cup)

1. Preheat the oven to 375°F and position a rack in the center.

*2. **Assemble the lasagna:*** Mix together ½ cup of the béchamel sauce and ¼ cup of room-temperature water and spread it in a 9 x 13-inch (3-quart) glass or ceramic baking dish, then top with one third of the noodles (2 sheets). Spread 1 cup of the béchamel sauce on the pasta and cover with 1½ cups of the Bolognese sauce. Sprinkle with ⅓ cup of the Parmesan. Repeat with another layer of noodles, 1 cup of the béchamel, the remaining Bolognese sauce, and ⅓ cup of the Parmesan. Top with the remaining noodles, béchamel, and Parmesan.

*3. **Bake the lasagna:*** Cover with foil and bake for 30 minutes. Uncover and bake until bubbling and the top is golden, about 20 minutes longer. Let rest for 15 minutes before cutting into squares and serving.

MOUSSAKA

When we asked Philadelphia chef Michael Solomonov about his favorite lasagna recipe, his answer was simple: moussaka. Skeptical as we were, it was hard to deny that the classic Greek dish has a number of lasagna hallmarks; after all, many historians speculate that lasagna has its roots in ancient Greece (see page 8). In this version, adapted from his award-winning cookbook *Zahav*, there are eggplant layers rather than pasta; ground beef cooked simply and quickly with onions, carrots, and cinnamon; and a spicy tomato sauce. Some classic versions include a top layer of béchamel, but in his, Michael avoids the mixture of milk and meat so that the dish is a little lighter (and potentially kosher).

Extra-virgin olive oil

1 medium yellow onion, diced (about 1 cup)

1 carrot, peeled and diced

1 pound ground beef (85% lean)

¾ teaspoon ground cinnamon

1½ teaspoons ground coriander

Coarse kosher salt (preferably Diamond Crystal) and freshly ground black pepper

1 medium eggplant (about 1¼ pounds), sliced crosswise ¼ inch thick on a mandoline or with a sharp knife

¼ cup chopped fresh flat-leaf parsley

1 cup Classic & Simple Red Sauce (page 130), warm

1. Make the meat mixture: Warm 1 tablespoon olive oil in a large skillet over medium heat. Add the onion and carrot and cook, stirring occasionally, until the vegetables have softened but not begun to brown, about 10 minutes. Add the beef, cinnamon, coriander, ¾ teaspoon salt, and ½ teaspoon pepper, stirring to incorporate, and continue cooking, breaking up the meat with a wooden spoon until the beef is cooked through and begins to brown, another 15 minutes. Remove from the heat.

2. Bake the eggplant: Preheat the oven to 400°F and position a rack in the center. Line a baking sheet with parchment paper. Brush each side of the eggplant slices with oil, using about ¼ cup in total. Arrange the slices on the prepared baking sheet and season with ¾ teaspoon salt. Bake until the eggplant softens, about 5 minutes. Lower the oven temperature to 350°F.

3. Bake the moussaka: Brush the bottom of a 9-inch glass or ceramic pie dish with oil and line it with the eggplant slices, leaving some to hang over the sides. Mix the parsley with the ground beef and spoon it over the eggplant. Top with the red sauce. Fold the overhanging eggplant over the filling. Drizzle the top with more oil. Bake until the top begins to brown in spots, about 30 minutes. Let the moussaka rest at room temperature for 30 minutes before slicing and serving. Or cool completely and reheat to serve.

2

NOT CLASSICS

We've seen every lasagna mash-up you can
possibly think of, from lasagna made with Cheetos to fish sticks and
even Snickers bars. But we're not in this game for the retweets and
likes. What we look for in an unclassic lasagna is the perfect middle
ground between stalwart recipe and one that makes us shriek with
excitement (and, obviously, it needs to taste great, too). In this
chapter, we convert meaty, peperoncini-stuffed Italian subs into
lasagna. We rethink northern Italy's beet-and-brown-butter ravioli
as something that can be baked into layers rather than boiled in
half-moon–shaped pouches. We swap out ricotta for creamy corn
purees and fry bite-size squares of lasagna into crispy, melty, late-
night snacks you can pop with a cold beer.

The Classics chapter (page 26–45) gave you a repertoire of basics
that will appease all the sticklers for tradition. Now it's time to
shake things up.

CARBONARA LASAGNA

Part of the fun of spaghetti carbonara is that it combines all the best parts of breakfast (like eggs, ham, and cheese) with the best parts of dinner (like pasta, and having time to actually eat a sit-down meal). This lasagna version of carbonara includes mild Fontina, pancetta-studded ricotta, and eggs baked right in, toad-in-the-hole style. It's as equally delicious served with a chilled bottle of Lambrusco on a Friday night, or for breakfast the next morning with cold brew.

1 tablespoon unsalted butter, plus more for the dish

12 ounces thick-sliced pancetta, cut into ¼-inch dice

2 medium shallots, halved and thinly sliced (about 1 cup)

1 pound ricotta cheese

4 ounces Fontina cheese, shredded (about 1 cup)

2 ounces freshly grated Parmesan cheese (about ½ cup)

1 tablespoon fresh thyme leaves, removed from the stem

1½ cups heavy cream

½ teaspoon coarse kosher salt (preferably Diamond Crystal)

¼ teaspoon freshly ground black pepper

1 recipe (12 sheets; about 12 ounces) Fresh Pasta Sheets (page 129), cooked

4 large eggs

1. Preheat the oven to 375°F with a rack in the lower third. Lightly butter an 8 x 11-inch (2-quart) glass or ceramic baking dish.

2. Make the cheese mixture: Melt 1 tablespoon butter in a large skillet over medium-high heat. Add the pancetta and cook, stirring occasionally, until most of the fat is rendered and the pancetta is golden, 8 to 10 minutes. Add the shallots and cook over medium heat, stirring, until softened, about 5 minutes. Using a slotted spoon, transfer the shallots and pancetta to a bowl. Let cool slightly, then stir in the ricotta, Fontina, and Parmesan.

3. Infuse the cream: Pour off the fat and return the skillet to medium-high heat. Stir in the thyme, then the heavy cream, scraping up the browned bits stuck to the pan. Bring just to a simmer and season with the salt and pepper. Remove from the heat.

4. Assemble the lasagna: Cut the noodles to fit the dish and arrange a layer of two in the bottom, overlapping slightly. Dollop with one quarter of the cheese mixture and top with another layer of noodles. Repeat three more times with the remaining filling and noodles, ending with a layer of noodles (you will have several leftover). Pour the cream over the lasagna. Shake the dish gently to distribute. Press with a spatula to compact slightly.

5. Bake the lasagna: Bake the lasagna until golden, about 40 minutes. Crack the eggs into individual bowls. Press a 2-inch round cookie cutter into the lasagna, going about halfway down. Carefully remove the top layers of lasagna to create a well. Repeat to create three more. Gently drop 1 egg in each well and return to the oven. Cover with foil and bake until the egg whites are just set, 5 to 7 minutes longer. Let rest for 15 minutes before serving.

A POTENTIALLY VEGAN PUTTANESCA LASAGNA

Spaghetti puttanesca is less of a pasta dish that hangs around in the background (looking at you, Alfredo) and more of a go-getter–a thwack of salt, brine, and spice. The dish, which originated in Naples, traditionally is made with spaghetti blanketed in a spicy tomato sauce spiked with an umami-packed trio of olives, capers, and anchovies. Since these core ingredients bring so much salty flavor, we decided to skip cheese when we transformed the dish into a lasagna. That means that if you leave the anchovies out and use a standard dried eggless pasta, you can actually make a vegan lasagna that won't make you sad.

5 tablespoons extra-virgin olive oil

1 medium yellow onion, finely chopped

3 large garlic cloves, finely chopped

6 large anchovies, finely chopped (or 1½ tablespoons anchovy paste)

¼ to ½ teaspoon dried red pepper flakes

1 teaspoon dried oregano

¼ cup tomato paste

1 (28-ounce) can whole peeled Italian tomatoes, with their juices

1 teaspoon sugar

2 large fresh basil sprigs

1 cup mixed pitted, sliced olives, such as Kalamata, Gaeta, Castelvetrano, and a combination of oil-cured and brined olives

2 tablespoons drained brined capers

Coarse kosher salt (preferably Diamond Crystal) and freshly ground black pepper

1 recipe (12 sheets; about 12 ounces) Fresh Pasta Sheets (page 129), cooked and cooled

1. Make the sauce: Preheat the oven to 375°F with a rack in the lower third. Heat 3 tablespoons of the oil in a 2- to 3-quart enameled cast-iron casserole or Dutch oven over medium-high heat. Add the onion, cover, and cook, stirring once or twice, until translucent, about 5 minutes. Add the garlic, anchovies, red pepper flakes, and oregano and cook, uncovered, stirring until fragrant, about 1 minute. Stir in the tomato paste and cook, stirring, until it darkens slightly, 1 to 2 minutes.

2. Add the whole peeled tomatoes, 1½ cups water, and the sugar and bring to a boil. Using a potato masher or wooden spoon, break up the tomatoes slightly. Reduce the heat to medium, add the basil sprigs, and simmer, uncovered, until reduced to 4½ cups, about 15 minutes. Stir in the olives and capers and simmer for 5 minutes longer. Season to taste with salt and black pepper and discard the basil sprigs.

3. Set a fine-mesh sieve over a bowl. Spoon the sauce into the sieve and shake gently to separate the solids from the liquids. Do not press; reserve the olive–tomato mixture separately.

4. Assemble the lasagna: Spoon a few tablespoons of the strained sauce into an 8 x 11-inch (2-quart) glass or ceramic baking dish. Cut the noodles to fit the dish and arrange one-fifth in the bottom, reserving the best-looking ones for the top layer. Spoon one quarter of the reserved olive–tomato mixture over the noodles (save the strained sauce for the top). Repeat with the remaining noodles and olive–tomato mixture, ending with the nicest noodles on top to create 5 layers of noodles and 4 layers of filling. Pour and spread the strained tomato sauce on top and drizzle generously with the remaining 2 tablespoons of olive oil.

5. Bake the lasagna: Cover with foil and bake for 25 minutes. Uncover and bake until the sauce is nearly absorbed and the top is browned in spots, 20 to 25 minutes longer. Let rest for 15 minutes before cutting and serving.

LASAGNA *with* KALE PESTO

Blitzing Tuscan kale into a pesto with basil, almonds, and anchovies offers a smooth, rich filling for this vegetable lasagna full of rustic cruciferous character. The anchovies here are barely noticeable, so don't sweat it if one of your dinner guests is not big on them or if you want to keep the whole dish vegetarian. The pesto recipe makes about one and a half cups; spread leftover pesto on grilled bread or fold it into roasted potatoes.

8-ounces of Tuscan or curly kale (4 packed cups of leaves)

¼ cup fresh basil leaves

2 large garlic cloves, finely chopped

¼ cup roasted, salted almonds (with or without skin)

6 flat anchovy fillets (optional)

¼ cup plus 2 tablespoons extra-virgin olive oil

½ teaspoon dried red pepper flakes

2 ounces freshly grated Pecorino Romano cheese (about ½ cup)

Coarse kosher salt (preferably Diamond Crystal) and freshly ground black pepper

2 pounds ricotta cheese

2 large eggs

1 pound low-moisture mozzarella cheese (not fresh), shredded (about 4 cups)

1 recipe (4½ cups) Classic & Simple Red Sauce (page 130), warm

15 dry lasagna noodles, cooked and cooled (see page 16)

1. **Make the kale pesto:** Preheat the oven to 375°F and position a rack in the center. Transfer half of the kale to a food processor. Add the basil, garlic, almonds, and anchovies, if using, and pulse until roughly chopped before adding the rest of the kale. With the machine running, add the oil in a steady stream, then add the red pepper flakes and ¼ cup of the Pecorino. Transfer to a small bowl and season with salt and black pepper.

2. **Make the cheese mixture:** Place the ricotta in a medium bowl and season with 2 teaspoons salt and ½ teaspoon black pepper. Stir in the eggs and half of the mozzarella. Swirl in ¾ cup of the pesto (or more to taste).

3. **Assemble the lasagna:** Spread ½ cup of the red sauce in the bottom of a 9 x 13-inch (3-quart) glass or ceramic baking dish. Arrange 5 of the noodles, overlapping slightly, in the dish. Spead half of the ricotta mixture onto the noodles. Top with 1½ cups of the sauce. Arrange another 5 noodles on top, followed by the remaining ricotta mixture and another 1½ cups sauce. Arrange the remaining noodles on top and spread with the remaining sauce.

4. **Bake the lasagna:** Sprinkle the remaining mozzarella and Pecorino Romano on top and bake until the top is browned and crusty around the edges and bubbling, about 45 minutes. Let the lasagna rest for 20 minutes before cutting into squares and serving.

EGGPLANT PARM LASAGNA

Eggplant parm is famously the dish that can convert even the staunchest of eggplant haters over to the bright side. The rustic, cheesy casserole lends itself wonderfully to a lasagna rethink, in which ricotta and sauce are spread between curly noodles and thin slices of roasted eggplant to create a textured, meatless pasta adventure. If you have leftover grilled eggplant from dinner a few nights ago, that will work, too, adding a cool element of smoke to the baked-pasta equation.

8 TO 12 SERVINGS

3 pounds Italian eggplant (about 3 medium), peeled and sliced into ¼-inch-thick rounds

¼ cup extra-virgin olive oil

Coarse kosher salt (preferably Diamond Crystal) and freshly ground black pepper

1 pound ricotta cheese

2 tablespoons chopped fresh flat-leaf parsley

1 large egg

1 pound low-moisture mozzarella cheese (not fresh), shredded (about 4 cups)

2 ounces freshly grated Pecorino Romano cheese (about ½ cup)

1 recipe (4½ cups) Classic & Simple Red Sauce (page 130), warm

15 dry lasagna noodles, cooked and cooled (see page 16)

1. Roast the eggplant: Preheat the broiler to high and place 2 racks in the upper third and lower third positions. Arrange the eggplant on 2 large baking sheets and brush both sides with the oil. Season with salt and pepper and broil one pan at a time on the upper rack, until the eggplant is browned and tender, about 10 minutes, flipping the slices midway through and shifting the pan as needed for even browning. Repeat with the second pan of eggplant, then heat the oven to 375°F.

2. Make the cheese mixture: In a medium bowl, combine the ricotta with the parsley, egg, half of the mozzarella, and ¼ cup of the Pecorino Romano. Season with 2 teaspoons salt and ½ teaspoon pepper.

3. Assemble the lasagna: Spread ½ cup of the red sauce in the bottom of a 9 x 13-inch

(3-quart) glass or ceramic baking dish. Arrange 5 of the noodles, overlapping slightly, in the dish. Spoon half of the ricotta mixture onto the noodles and spread an even layer. Top with one third of the eggplant and 1 cup of the sauce. Repeat with another layer of 5 noodles, the remaining ricotta mixture, and half of the remaining eggplant. Spoon 1 cup of the sauce over the eggplant, and top with the remaining noodles. Spread ½ cup of sauce over the noodles and top with the remaining eggplant and sauce.

4. Sprinkle the remaining mozzarella and Pecorino Romano on top and bake on the lower oven rack until the top is browned and crusty around the edges and bubbling, about 45 minutes. Let the lasagna rest for 20 minutes before cutting into squares and serving.

BEET-RICOTTA LASAGNA
with BROWN BUTTER & POPPY SEEDS

In Veneto, a region in northeast Italy famous for its sprawling fields of bright red poppies, half-moon–shaped ravioli known as *casunziei* are often filled with beets and tossed in a nutty sauce made from butter and poppy seeds. This recipe echoes those ravioli, layering magenta, beet-stained ricotta with fresh pasta and sautéed beet stems and leaves. Rather than finishing the whole thing off with more cheese, the top layer here gets a load of brown butter, cream, and poppy seeds before going into the oven to toast.

5 tablespoons unsalted butter, plus more for the dish

2 red beets with green tops (about 1½ pounds)

1 tablespoon extra-virgin olive oil

½ cup finely chopped shallots

Coarse kosher salt (preferably Diamond Crystal) and freshly ground black pepper

1½ cups heavy cream

1 teaspoon finely grated lemon zest

1½ pounds ricotta cheese (3 cups)

1 large egg

¾ recipe (9 sheets; about 12 ounces) Fresh Pasta Sheets (page 129), cooked

4 ounces Taleggio cheese, rind removed, thinly sliced

1 tablespoon poppy seeds

1. **Prepare the beets:** Preheat the oven to 375°F with a rack in the lower third. Butter an 8 x 11-inch (2-quart) glass or ceramic baking dish. Cut the tops from the beets and separate the leaves from the stems. Finely chop the stems and set aside. Stack the leaves, then roll them like a cigar and cut crosswise into thin ribbons. Peel the beets and grate them on the large holes of a box grater or using the shredder attachment of a food processor (you should have about 2 cups of shredded beets).

2. **Sauté the beet greens:** In a large skillet set over medium-high heat, melt 1 tablespoon of the butter in the oil. Add the beat stems and leaves and half the shallots then season with a pinch of salt and pepper, and cook until soft, about 7 minutes, stirring occasionally. Transfer the mixture to a small bowl and stir in 2 tablespoons of the cream. Season to taste with salt and pepper.

3. Add 2 tablespoons of the butter to the skillet along with the remaining shallots and the grated beets, season with salt and pepper, and cook until completely tender and dry, 8 to 10 minutes. Transfer the mixture to a large bowl and stir in the lemon zest and ricotta. Season generously with salt and pepper, then stir in the egg.

4. Assemble the lasagna: Using 2 sheets per layer, cut the noodles to fit the dish and set a layer of noodles in the bottom, overlapping slightly. Spread with half of the beet-ricotta mixture and top with another layer of noodles. Top with the greens and Taleggio and another layer of noodles, followed by the remaining beet-ricotta mixture and a final layer of noodles.

5. Rinse out the skillet and add the remaining butter. Cook over medium-high heat, swirling the pan, until the butter starts to brown, about 5 minutes. Stir in the poppy seeds and remaining heavy cream. Season generously with salt and pour over the lasagna. Shake the dish gently to distribute. Bake until golden and bubbling, about 45 minutes. Let rest for 20 minutes before serving.

ACCIDENTALLY VEGAN SWEET CORN & SCALLION LASAGNA

Corn has such a naturally buttery, creamy flavor that in this recipe we decided to get crazy and skip the cheese layer of lasagna. By sautéing the corn and scallions and blending them together, you create a puree that eliminates the need for béchamel or ricotta. The result is an unbelievably bright, fresh, accidentally vegan lasagna full of rich sweet-corn flavor, topped with juicy cherry tomatoes and green pesto. If you miss the cheese, you can add a little bit of Parmesan to your pesto, or you can do what we did and add a pinch of nutritional yeast to give it a nutty saltiness that will play off the toasted pine nuts.

Lasagna

4 ears corn, shucked

¾ cup plus 2 tablespoons grapeseed oil

½ medium white onion, chopped (about ½ cup)

1 bunch of scallions, thinly sliced, keeping whites and pale greens separate from the green tops

2 tablespoons all-purpose flour

Coarse kosher salt (preferably Diamond Crystal) and freshly ground black pepper

12 no-boil lasagna noodles (see Note), or ½ recipe (6 sheets; about 8 ounces) Fresh Pasta Sheets (page 129), cooked

1 pint mixed cherry tomatoes (preferably heirloom), quartered

Pesto

¼ cup pine nuts, (preferably Italian)

1 cup fresh basil leaves, plus more for garnish

2 large garlic cloves, smashed

1½ tablespoons nutritional yeast (optional)

NOTE
If using dried, curly noodles, arrange 15 preboiled noodles in 3 layers and bake uncovered the entire time.

1. Prepare the corn: Preheat the oven to 375°F with a rack in the center. Stand an ear of corn upright on a work surface and slice the kernels from the cob. Transfer the kernels to a medium bowl (you should have about 3 cups). In another wide bowl, stand the cob upright and using the spine of a table knife, scrape the cob to extract the corn pulp (milk). Repeat with the remaining ears of corn (you should end up with about 2 tablespoons of corn pulp).

2. Place the scraped cobs in a large saucepan with 4 cups water and bring to a boil over high heat. Reduce the heat to medium, cover, and simmer for 15 minutes.

(recipe continues)

3. In a large skillet, heat the 2 tablespoons of oil over medium-high heat until shimmering, about 2 minutes. Add the onion and cook over medium-high heat, stirring occasionally, until translucent, 3 to 5 minutes. Add the corn kernels (not the pulp) and cook until translucent, about 3 minutes. Add the scallion whites and pale greens and cook until fragrant, about 1 minute. Transfer half of the mixture to a bowl, stir in most of the scallion green tops (save some for serving), and set aside.

4. To the corn in the skillet, add the flour and cook over medium-high heat, while stirring, until pale golden, about 1 minute. Add 2 cups of the corn broth and cook, whisking constantly, until slightly thickened, about 3 minutes. Stir in the corn pulp, then scrape the mixture into a blender. Cover the blender bowl with a kitchen towel (this will create a vent for the steam), then top with the lid. Remove the feed tube and carefully puree until smooth. Season with 1 teaspoon salt and ¼ teaspoon pepper. Add enough of the remaining corn broth to equal 2¾ cups corn sauce.

5. *Assemble and bake the lasagna:* Spread ½ cup of the corn sauce on the bottom of a 9-inch (2½-quart) square glass or ceramic baking dish. Arrange a layer of 3 slightly overlapping lasagna noodles on top followed by one third of the corn–scallion mixture. Spoon ½ cup corn sauce on top, then repeat 2 more layers, each with 3 lasagna noodles, half of the corn–scallion mixture, and another ½ cup sauce. Finish with a layer of 3 more noodles, and pour the remaining sauce on top. Cover with foil, and bake for 25 minutes. Uncover and bake until bubbling and lightly golden, 15 minutes longer.

6. *Make the pesto:* Meanwhile, spread the pine nuts on a baking sheet and toast in the oven until golden, about 5 minutes. Transfer to a blender or food processor and let cool. Add the basil and garlic, and process until chopped. Add the remaining ¾ cup of oil and process the pesto until almost smooth. Add the nutritional yeast (if desired) and pulse to combine. Season with a pinch each of salt and pepper.

7. *Make the tomato salad:* In a small bowl, toss the tomatoes with a few tablespoons of the pesto and a generous pinch of salt and pepper. Let the lasagna rest for 15 minutes before cutting into squares and serving. Spoon some tomato salad on top, drizzle with additional pesto, and garnish with the reserved scallion greens and basil leaves.

ITALIAN SUB LASAGNA

When cookbook author, radio host, and *TASTE* contributor Cathy Erway told us about the Italian sub–inspired lasagna she occasionally makes for her Brooklyn dinner parties, we were mad at ourselves for not thinking of it first. Because of course: If capicola, peperoncini, Provolone, and sliced tomatoes taste good doused in oil and vinegar and wedged into a crusty sandwich roll, then why wouldn't they taste good baked between layers of pasta, with a touch of tomato sauce and ricotta to hold it all together? An unexpected bonus that we discovered when we tried out Cathy's New Jersey childhood–inspired lasagna for ourselves is that any leftover ingredients from the filling create a kind of accidental charcuterie platter.

1 pound ricotta cheese

1 large egg

½ teaspoon coarse kosher salt (preferably Diamond Crystal)

¼ teaspoon freshly ground black pepper

3 cups Classic & Simple Red Sauce (page 130), warm

12 dry lasagna noodles, cooked and cooled (see page 16), or ¾ recipe (9 sheets; about 12 ounces) Fresh Pasta Sheets (page 129), cooked

¼ pound sliced Genoa salami

¼ pound sliced pepperoni

¼ pound sliced mortadella or ham

¼ pound sliced capicola or bresaola

½ pound sliced Provolone cheese

About 12 peperoncini, sliced into thin rings

2 large beefsteak tomatoes, cored and sliced into ¼-inch-thick rounds

1 medium green bell pepper, halved, cored, seeded, and thinly sliced

1 medium white onion, thinly sliced

½ teaspoon dried oregano

4 tablespoons extra-virgin olive oil

About 4 ounces grated Parmigiano-Reggiano cheese (1 cup)

About 8 ounces grated mozzarella cheese (2 cups)

1. Make the cheese mixture: Preheat the oven to 350°F with the rack in the center. In a medium bowl, mix the ricotta with the egg, salt, and pepper.

2. Assemble the lasagna: Spread a small ladleful of red sauce on the bottom of a 9 x 13-inch (3-quart) glass or ceramic baking dish. Arrange a layer of 3 slightly overlapping lasagna noodles on top. Arrange one third of

(recipe continues)

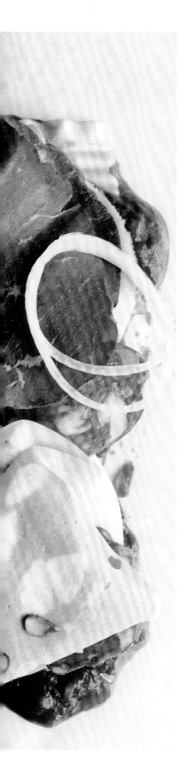

the sliced salami on top of the pasta. Repeat with one third of the pepperoni, mortadella, and capicola. Cover with one third of the Provolone, then with one third of the peperoncini, tomatoes, bell pepper, and onion. Sprinkle with a pinch of the oregano and a drizzle of the olive oil.

3. Top with another layer of 3 noodles. Spread one third of the ricotta mixture evenly across the top (alternately, use a piping bag to pipe an even layer of ricotta). Sprinkle the top with 1 to 2 tablespoons of the Parmigiano-Reggiano and a generous pinch of the oregano. Top it with another layer of pasta. Spread 1 cup of the red sauce across this layer, and cover the layer with half of the remaining deli meats, Provolone, and sliced vegetables. Repeat the ricotta layer and add a final layer of deli meats, a final layer of Provolone, and a final ricotta layer.

4. *Bake the lasagna:* Spread the final addition of the pasta sheets with the remaining sauce, followed by the grated mozzarella, remaining Parmigiano-Reggiano, and another pinch of oregano. Cover the lasagna tightly with foil and bake for about 30 minutes.

5. Remove the foil and continue baking for another 10 minutes, or until the top is slightly browned. Let cool for about 20 minutes before serving.

SWEET PEA LASAGNA *with* MINT PESTO

Usually when you encounter a green lasagna, it's the one measly vegetarian dish on the counter at the potluck. Or it's served on Saint Patrick's Day, when random foods weirdly turn green for the day. But boy, do we have the green lasagna for you. In this recipe, there's not a leafy green in sight–just a grassy-green sweet pea and leek puree, stirred into ricotta and alternated with handfuls of tender asparagus and leeks. Lemon zest and a finish of mint oil makes the whole thing a bright and refreshing counterpoint to challenge the meat-and-cheese-bomb lasagna stereotypes.

3 tablespoons unsalted butter, plus more for the dish

2 large leeks (about 1 pound), white and green parts, trimmed, halved lengthwise, and cut into 1-inch pieces, washed well and drained

Coarse kosher salt (preferably Diamond Crystal) and freshly ground black pepper

2 cups frozen baby peas (10 ounces), thawed

1½ pounds ricotta cheese (3 cups)

1 teaspoon finely grated lemon zest, plus lemon wedges for serving

1 large egg

1 pound medium asparagus, bottom 2 inches snapped off, spears cut into 1-inch pieces

¾ recipe (9 sheets; about 12 ounces) Fresh Pasta Sheets (page 129), cooked and cooled

4 ounces Taleggio cheese, rind removed, thinly sliced

1½ cups heavy cream

¾ cup fresh mint leaves

½ cup neutral oil, such as grapeseed

1. Preheat the oven to 375°F with a rack in the lower third. Butter an 8 x 11-inch (2-quart) glass or ceramic baking dish.

2. Make the cheese mixture: In a large skillet, melt 2 tablespoons of the butter. Add the leeks and season with salt and pepper. Cover and cook over medium heat, stirring occasionally, until softened, about 8 minutes. Transfer half of the leeks to a plate and add the other half to a food processor. Add the peas to the food processor and puree until smooth. Transfer the pea-leek mixture to a large bowl and stir in the ricotta and lemon zest. Season with 1 teaspoon salt and ¼ teaspoon pepper, then stir in the egg.

3. Cook the asparagus: Melt the remaining tablespoon of butter in the skillet. Add the asparagus, season with salt and pepper, and cook, stirring occasionally, until crisp-tender, 3 to 4 minutes. Transfer to the plate with the leeks.

4. Assemble the lasagna: Using 2 sheets per layer, cut the noodles to fit the dish and arrange a layer, overlapping slightly, in the bottom. Spread with half of the pea–ricotta

(recipe continues)

mixture and top with another layer of noodles. Top with the sautéed leeks and asparagus. Arrange the Taleggio on top and then add another layer of noodles. Spread with the remaining pea–ricotta mixture and top with a final layer of noodles.

5. *Bake the lasagna:* Add the cream to the skillet and bring just to a boil. Season generously with salt and pepper and pour over the lasagna. Shake the dish gently to distribute the cream. Bake until golden and bubbling, about 45 minutes. Let rest for 20 minutes.

6. Meanwhile, rinse out the food processor. Add the mint and oil and puree until smooth. Season with salt and pepper. Cut the lasagna into squares, drizzle with the mint oil, and serve with lemon wedges. (Alternatively, omit the mint oil and garnish with fresh chopped mint leaves and a drizzle of oil.)

ROASTED SQUASH LASAGNA
with LEEKS **&** SAGE

Do you ever think about how unjust it is that ravioli gets all the airtime when it comes to butternut squash pastas? In this lasagna, we decided to think of squash as its own textural element—cut into little cubes and roasted in a good amount of butter and olive oil until the sides are caramelized and crisp and the insides are creamy. Justice is served.

2 tablespoons unsalted butter, plus more for the dish

2 tablespoons extra-virgin olive oil

2 pounds peeled and cubed (1-inch) butternut squash (from a 4-pound squash)

Coarse kosher salt (preferably Diamond Crystal) and freshly ground black pepper

2 large leeks (about 1 pound), white and green parts, trimmed, halved lengthwise, and cut into 1-inch pieces, washed well and drained

1 tablespoon chopped fresh sage leaves, plus 12 whole leaves for the top

1 recipe (4 cups) Classic Béchamel (page 139)

15 dry lasagna noodles, cooked and cooled (see page 16)

½ cup freshly grated Parmesan cheese

8 ounces Monterey Jack cheese, shredded (2 cups)

1. Roast the squash: Preheat the oven to 425°F with a rack in the center. In a skillet, melt the butter in the oil over medium heat. Arrange the squash on a rimmed baking sheet and toss with half of the butter-oil mixture, salt, and pepper. Roast, stirring once, until the squash is tender and browned in spots, about 30 minutes.

2. Cook the leeks: Add the leeks to the skillet with the remaining butter-oil mixture and season with salt and pepper. Cover and cook over medium heat, stirring occasionally, until softened and bright green, about 5 minutes. Stir in the chopped sage and cook until fragrant, about 1 minute.

3. Assemble the lasagna: Lower the oven temperature to 375°F. Spread ½ cup of the béchamel in a 9 x 13-inch (3-quart) glass or

ceramic baking dish. Arrange 5 of the noodles on top, overlapping slightly; spread with 1 cup of the béchamel and sprinkle with one third of the Parmesan. Top with half each of the squash, leeks, and Monterey Jack. Repeat with another layer of 5 noodles, another 1 cup of béchamel, another third of the Parmesan, and the remaining squash, leeks, and Monterey Jack. Top with the remaining 5 noodles and the remaining 1½ cups of béchamel, spreading to an even layer. Arrange the whole sage leaves on top and sprinkle with the remaining Parmesan.

4. Bake the lasagna: Cover with foil and bake for 20 minutes. Uncover and bake until top is beginning to brown, about 15 minutes. Turn on the broiler until the top is golden, about 2 minutes longer. Let rest for 15 minutes before serving.

RED WINE-BRAISED SHORT RIB LASAGNA

In Italy, short rib ragus are often ladled over flat and wide pastas like pappardelle or tagliatelle. We decided to serve this one over an even wider pasta: lasagna noodles. The magic happens when you marinate the short ribs in red wine, garlic, and bay leaves, then braise them slowly until the meat falls off the bones in delicate shreds. The reduced mixture of fat, wine, and aromatics becomes a sauce that gets absorbed into the pasta and béchamel as the lasagna bakes. These short ribs are so flavorful on their own that if you double the recipe, you can spoon them over bowls of couscous or polenta for dinner one night and turn them into a lasagna later in the week.

2 cups semidry red wine, such as Cabernet Sauvignon, Malbec, or Bordeaux

6 fresh thyme sprigs

6 large garlic cloves, smashed

2 dried bay leaves

½ teaspoon whole black peppercorns

3 pounds bone-in English-cut short ribs (bones cut lengthwise), trimmed of visible fat

Coarse kosher salt (preferably Diamond Crystal) and freshly ground black pepper

1 tablespoon extra-virgin olive oil, plus more for the dish

2 large shallots, thinly sliced (1 cup)

¼ cup tomato paste

2 cups beef broth

½ cup freshly grated Parmesan cheese

1 recipe (4 cups) Thick Béchamel (see page 139)

2 large eggs

15 dry lasagna noodles, cooked and cooled (see page 16)

1. Marinate the short ribs: Put the wine in a large resealable plastic bag along with the thyme, garlic, bay leaves, and peppercorns. Add the short ribs, being careful not to pierce the bag with the bones. Seal the bag, pressing out as much air as possible. Set aside at room temperature for 2 hours, or, if marinating for more than 2 hours, refrigerate up to overnight, turning the bag occasionally.

2. Preheat the oven to 350°F with a rack in the lower third. Set a colander over a large bowl and carefully strain the short ribs (save the marinade for later). Pick out and reserve the thyme and bay leaves (discard the garlic and peppercorns). Place the short ribs on a plate and use a paper towel to pat them dry, then season them all over with 1 teaspoon salt and ¼ teaspoon pepper.

(recipe continues)

3. Cook the short ribs: Heat the oil in a large, deep, ovenproof Dutch oven over medium heat until shimmering, about 2 minutes. Add the short ribs and cook, turning occasionally, until deeply browned and crusty all over, 10 to 13 minutes. Transfer the short ribs to a large bowl and set aside. Pour off all but 1 tablespoon of the fat in the Dutch oven and discard.

4. Add the shallots to the remaining fat and cook over medium heat, stirring occasionally, until softened, about 5 minutes. Stir in the tomato paste and cook, stirring, until it darkens slightly, 1 to 2 minutes. Add the broth, the strained marinade, and the reserved thyme and bay leaves, and bring to a boil. Return the short ribs to the Dutch oven (it's okay if the liquid does not cover the ribs). Press a round of parchment paper directly onto the ribs (this creates a barrier for the moisture, which allows the liquid to evaporate slowly) and place the pot in the oven. Braise until the meat is very tender and falling off the bone, turning the ribs occasionally for even cooking, about 2 hours.

5. Transfer the ribs to a plate and use a spoon to skim off as much of the fat from the sauce as possible. There should be about 1 cup of defatted sauce. Discard the thyme and bay leaves. Remove and discard the bones from the short ribs, as well as any tough bits. Cut the meat into 1-inch pieces and pull it apart into thick shreds. Stir the meat into the sauce in the pot.

6. Make the Parmesan béchamel: Increase the oven temperature to 375°F and lightly oil a 9 x 13-inch (3-quart) glass or ceramic baking dish. Stir ¼ cup of the Parmesan into the béchamel. Spoon 1 cup of the béchamel into a bowl and whisk in the eggs. Whisk the egg mixture back into the remaining béchamel.

7. Assemble the lasagna: Arrange 5 of the noodles, overlapping slightly, in the dish. Spoon half of the meat sauce onto the noodles. Top with 1¼ cups of the béchamel, spreading to an even layer. Arrange another 5 noodles on top, followed by the remaining meat sauce and another 1¼ cups béchamel. Arrange the remaining noodles on top and spread with the remaining béchamel.

8. Bake the lasagna: Sprinkle the remaining Parmesan on top and bake until the top is browned and crusty around the edges and bubbling, about 45 minutes. Let the lasagna rest for 20 minutes before cutting into squares and serving.

PORCHETTA-SPICED PORK SHOULDER LASAGNA

In central Italy, hulking pork roasts known as *porchetta* are cooked for hours with rosemary, fennel, and garlic and sold as a street food–the juicy slices shaved onto sandwiches. In Philadelphia, you can find this pork on sandwiches full of broccoli rabe and Provolone. But making *porchetta* at home is a bit of a production. It involves brining, rubbing, rolling, and tying a large cut of pork belly–all before it actually goes in the oven. In this recipe, we channel *porchetta*'s dreamy personality (and juiciness and spices) with a simple pork shoulder that gets braised in white wine, creating a tender shredded filling for a red sauce lasagna.

Porchetta-Spiced Pork

4 tablespoons extra-virgin olive oil

2½ pounds trimmed boneless pork shoulder, cut into 1-inch pieces

1 teaspoon coarse kosher salt (preferably Diamond Crystal)

¼ teaspoon freshly ground black pepper

2 large garlic cloves, chopped

1½ tablespoons fennel seeds

1½ tablespoons chopped fresh rosemary

½ teaspoon dried red pepper flakes

½ cup dry white wine

3 cups low-sodium chicken broth

2 dried bay leaves

Lasagna

2 pounds ricotta cheese (about 4 cups)

2 tablespoons finely chopped fresh flat-leaf parsley

2 ounces freshly grated Parmesan cheese (½ cup)

1 pound low-moisture mozzarella cheese (not fresh), shredded (4 cups)

2 teaspoons coarse kosher salt (preferably Diamond Crystal)

½ teaspoon freshly ground black pepper

1 large egg, beaten

4 cups Classic & Simple Red Sauce (page 130), warm

15 dry, curly lasagna noodles, cooked and cooled (see page 16)

(recipe continues)

*1. **Make the porchetta-spiced pork:***
In a medium Dutch oven or enameled cast-iron casserole, heat 2 tablespoons of the oil over medium heat until shimmering, about 2 minutes. Season the pork with the salt and black pepper and cook in batches, turning the pieces as needed, until they are browned and crusty all over, 8 to 10 minutes. Transfer the browned pork to a plate with a slotted spoon and brown the remaining meat, adding the remaining 2 tablespoons of oil to the pot. Transfer to the plate when done.

2. Meanwhile, place the chopped garlic, fennel seeds, and chopped rosemary on a cutting board and continue to chop them together until uniformly fine. Add the mixture, along with the red pepper flakes, to the pot used to cook the pork, and cook over medium heat, stirring, until fragrant, about 1 minute.

3. Add the wine and cook until reduced by half, 2 to 3 minutes. Return the meat to the pot along with any accumulated juices. Add the broth and bay leaves and bring to a boil. Reduce the heat to medium low and simmer, partially covered, until the pork is very tender, about 1 hour. Discard the bay leaves and transfer the pork to a bowl. Spoon off as much fat from the surface as possible and boil the remaining liquid over medium-low heat until reduced to a few tablespoons, 5 to 6 minutes. Return the pork to the pot and

cook, stirring, over low heat until the liquid is nearly evaporated, about 3 minutes. Use a wooden spoon to press on the pork and coarsely shred it.

*4. **Make the cheese mixture:*** Preheat the oven to 375°F. In a large bowl, combine the ricotta, parsley, ¼ cup of the Parmesan, and two thirds of the mozzarella (reserve the remaining cheese for the top) and season with the salt and black pepper. Add the egg and stir to combine.

*5. **Assemble the lasagna:*** Spread ½ cup of the red sauce in the bottom of a 9 x 13-inch (3-quart) glass or ceramic baking dish. Arrange 5 of the noodles, overlapping slightly, in the dish. Top with ½ cup of the red sauce. Spoon half of the ricotta mixture on top, spreading to an even layer. Top with half of the shredded pork. Arrange another 5 noodles on top, followed by another ½ cup red sauce, the remaining ricotta mixture, and the remaining pork. Arrange the remaining noodles on top, pressing to compact slightly, and spread with 1½ cups red sauce.

*6. **Bake the lasagna:*** Sprinkle the remaining mozzarella and Parmesan on top and bake until the top is browned and crusty around the edges and bubbling, about 45 minutes. Let the lasagna rest for 20 minutes before cutting into squares. Serve the remaining red sauce on the side.

SPEEDY SKILLET RAVIOLI LASAGNA

This is our version of lasagna in under thirty minutes: Thanks to a little help from a package of frozen ravioli, you can pull a skillet of toasty, bubbly lasagna from the oven in a little more than half an hour. In this ingenious one pan supper (shout-out to Grace Parisi, the brains behind the recipe!), you make a tomato sauce right in the same skillet you use to bake the whole thing, and the ravioli–layered with mozzarella and Parm–cooks and soaks up the tomato flavor at the same time the starch from the pasta thickens the sauce. Now, Grace, can you please work on an air-fryer lasagna recipe for *Lasagna*, the sequel?

Tomato Sauce

2 tablespoons extra-virgin olive oil	Pinch of dried red pepper flakes	1 teaspoon sugar
2 large garlic cloves, thinly sliced	1 (28-ounce) can crushed tomatoes	1 teaspoon coarse kosher salt (preferably Diamond Crystal)
2 tablespoons tomato paste	2 large fresh basil sprigs, plus torn leaves for garnish	¼ teaspoon freshly ground black pepper

Lasagna

1½ pounds frozen cheese ravioli	8 ounces mozzarella cheese (preferably fresh), shredded (2 cups)	2 tablespoons freshly grated Parmesan cheese

1. Make the tomato sauce: Preheat the oven to 450°F with a rack in the center. Heat the oil in a large ovenproof skillet over medium heat until shimmering, about 2 minutes. Add the garlic and cook, stirring, until softened but not browned, 1 to 2 minutes. Add the tomato paste and cook, stirring, until it darkens slightly, 1 to 2 minutes. Add the red pepper flakes, crushed tomatoes, basil sprigs, sugar, and 1 cup water. Season with the salt and black pepper and increase the heat slightly to bring to a boil.

2. Cook the ravioli: Gently separate any frozen ravioli stuck together without tearing. Any that resist will separate during cooking.

Add the ravioli to the skillet and cook over medium heat, stirring gently, until the sauce is very thick and the ravioli are just tender, about 15 minutes.

3. Assemble the ravioli lasagna: Spoon half of the ravioli and sauce into a bowl. Arrange the ravioli in the skillet in an even layer and sprinkle with half of the mozzarella. Arrange the remaining ravioli on top and sprinkle with the Parmesan and remaining mozzarella.

4. Bake the ravioli lasagna: Bake until bubbling and the cheese is lightly browned, 10 to 12 minutes. Scatter the basil leaves on top and let rest for 10 minutes before serving.

SPINACH ARTICHOKE DIP LASAGNA

8
SERVINGS

Why should spinach artichoke dip be confined to holiday parties and TGI Fridays when the melty, cream cheese–rich masterpiece makes a perfect pasta filling? In this recipe, lemon zest and red pepper flakes amp up mild cream cheese and Taleggio. The toasty tops and corners of the pasta give you the contrasting crunch you would get from those little baguette rounds at the party.

2 tablespoons
unsalted butter

1 tablespoon
extra-virgin olive oil

1 medium yellow onion,
chopped

2 (14-ounce) cans quartered
artichoke hearts, drained
and patted dry

1 teaspoon finely grated
lemon zest

Pinch of dried
red pepper flakes

Coarse kosher salt
(preferably Diamond
Crystal) and freshly ground
black pepper

10 ounces baby spinach

12 ounces cream cheese,
at room temperature

½ cup mayonnaise

15 dry lasagna noodles,
cooked and cooled
(see page 16), with 2 cups
pasta water reserved

12 ounces Taleggio cheese,
rind removed, cheese
broken into bite-size pieces
(or 12 ounces shredded
Fontina cheese)

¼ cup freshly grated
Parmesan cheese

1. **Cook the artichokes:** Preheat the oven to 375°F and position a rack in the center. In a large skillet, melt the butter in the oil over high heat. Add the onion and artichokes and cook, stirring occasionally, until the onion is soft and beginning to brown, 8 to 10 minutes. Stir in the lemon zest and red pepper flakes and season with salt and black pepper. Transfer the mixture to a bowl.

2. **Cook the spinach:** Return the skillet to medium-high heat. Add ¼ cup water and half of the spinach and stir until it begins to wilt. Add the second batch, stirring, until all of the spinach is wilted, about 30 seconds. Strain any excess liquid and gently stir the spinach into the artichoke mixture. Season to taste with salt and black pepper. Rinse out the skillet.

3. Off the heat, add the cream cheese, mayonnaise, and reserved pasta water to the skillet, whisking until smooth. Season with salt and black pepper.

4. **Assemble the lasagna:** Spread ½ cup of the cream cheese sauce in the bottom of a 9 x 13-inch (3-quart) glass or ceramic baking dish. Arrange 5 of the noodles, overlapping slightly, in the dish. Spoon half of the spinach–artichoke mixture onto the noodles in an even layer. Top with half of the Taleggio and ¾ cup of the sauce. Arrange another 5 noodles on top, followed by the remaining spinach–artichoke mixture, Taleggio, and another ¾ cup of the sauce. Top with the remaining 5 noodles and pour the remaining sauce on top, spreading evenly. Sprinkle with Parmesan.

5. Cover with foil and bake for 30 minutes. Uncover and bake until bubbling and golden, about 20 minutes longer. Let rest for 15 minutes before serving.

MOROCCAN-SPICED LAMB LASAGNA

The lamb filling in this lasagna might remind you of a Moroccan tagine or pastilla, or even that batch of gingerbread you made last winter. That's because the garlicky ground lamb is warmed with cinnamon and coated in a fruity, orange zest–laced tomato sauce. The sweet spices play off a generous layer of thick, nutmeg-y béchamel that's spread across the top and browned.

8 TO 12
SERVINGS

2 tablespoons
extra-virgin olive oil

1 medium yellow onion,
finely chopped

2 large garlic cloves,
finely chopped

2 pounds ground lamb

Coarse kosher salt
(preferably Diamond
Crystal) and freshly
ground black pepper

1 tablespoon chopped
fresh thyme

1½ teaspoons ground
cinnamon

⅓ cup tomato paste

1 teaspoon finely grated
orange zest

¾ cup freshly grated
Pecorino Romano cheese

1 recipe (4 cups) Thick
Béchamel (see page 139)

12 no-boil lasagna sheets
(from 1 box; see Note)

1. Cook the lamb: Preheat the oven to 375°F with a rack in the lower third. Heat the oil in a large skillet over medium-high heat until shimmering, about 2 minutes. Add the onion and cook, stirring occasionally, until translucent. Add the garlic and cook for 1 minute. Add the lamb and a pinch of salt and pepper and cook, breaking it into small pieces as you stir it, until the liquid is evaporated and the lamb is beginning to brown, 8 to 10 minutes. Add the thyme and cinnamon and cook until fragrant, about 1 minute. Stir in the tomato paste and cook, until it darkens slightly, 1 to 2 minutes.

2. Add 3 cups water and bring to a boil, scraping up any bits stuck to the bottom of the pan. Lower the heat to medium and simmer until the sauce is thick and has reduced to 6 cups, 25 to 30 minutes. Stir in the orange zest and season with salt and pepper.

3. Stir ½ cup of the Pecorino Romano into the béchamel. Set a fine-mesh sieve over a 9 x 13-inch (3-quart) glass or ceramic baking dish. Spoon 1 cup of the meat sauce into the strainer and press to extract as much liquid as possible into the baking dish. Return the meat to the skillet.

4. Assemble the lasagna: Arrange 3 of the oven-ready noodles in the baking dish. The noodles will expand to fit the dish. Spoon one third of the meat sauce over the noodles and 1 cup of the béchamel sauce. Repeat with 3 more noodles, another third of the meat sauce, and 1 cup of béchamel. Top with another 3 noodles and the remaining meat sauce. Top with the final 3 noodles and remaining béchamel, spreading to cover.

5. Bake the lasagna: Sprinkle with the remaining Pecorino Romano, cover with foil, and bake for 40 minutes. Uncover and bake until bubbling and the top is lightly golden, about 15 minutes longer. Let rest for 15 minutes before serving.

NOTE
*If using dried,
curly noodles,
arrange
15 preboiled
noodles in
3 layers and bake
uncovered the
entire time.*

SAUSAGE-FENNEL LASAGNA ROLLS

Sending someone a dozen roses is a nice thing to do. But serving them a dozen sausage-filled lasagna rosettes? Now that's true love. These cheesy rolls have all the makings of a classic lasagna, but rather than layering them all horizontally, we're rolling these curly noodles around caramelized fennel and Italian sausage to create pleasing spirals that sit snugly together like a beautiful bouquet.

2 tablespoons extra-virgin olive oil

1 pound sweet Italian fennel sausage, casings removed

1½ teaspoons finely grated lemon zest

½ teaspoon finely chopped fresh rosemary

1 large fennel bulb (1½ pounds), cut into ½-inch pieces

1 medium yellow onion, cut into ½-inch pieces

½ teaspoon coarse kosher salt (preferably Diamond Crystal)

¼ teaspoon freshly ground black pepper

½ cup freshly grated Parmesan cheese

1 pound Fontina cheese, shredded (about 4 cups)

1 recipe (4 cups) Classic Béchamel (page 139), warm

15 dry lasagna noodles, cooked and cooled (see page 16)

1. **Cook the sausage:** Preheat the oven to 375°F with a rack in the center. Heat the oil in a large skillet over high heat until shimmering, about 2 minutes. Add the sausage and cook, breaking it into very small pieces with a wooden spoon, until browned and cooked through, 8 to 10 minutes. Using a slotted spoon, transfer the sausage to a medium bowl and stir in the lemon zest and rosemary.

2. **Make the cheese mixture:** Add the fennel and onion to the skillet. Cover and cook over medium-low heat until softened, stirring occasionally, 8 to 10 minutes. Remove the lid and cook, stirring occasionally, until lightly browned, 10 to 12 minutes. Add a few tablespoons of water to the skillet from time to time, as needed, to prevent sticking. Season with the salt and pepper and add to the sausage. Stir in half of the Parmesan and two thirds of the Fontina.

3. **Assemble the lasagna rolls:** Spread ½ cup of the béchamel in the bottom of an 8 x 11-inch (2-quart) glass or ceramic baking dish. Arrange the noodles on a clean work surface side by side, vertically. Brush a very thin layer of béchamel on the noodles, then divide the sausage–fennel filling evenly among them. Starting at the bottom, roll each noodle away from you as tightly as possible to create a spiral. Set each roll in the baking dish side by side snugly so that they don't unravel. Tuck in any stray filling.

4. **Bake the lasagna rolls:** Pour the remaining béchamel all over and sprinkle with the remaining Parmesan and Fontina. Bake until golden and bubbling, about 45 minutes. Let rest for 20 minutes before serving.

LEFTOVER LASAGNA PARM SANDWICH

Call it crazy or call it carb-y, but leftover lasagna makes a great sandwich. Like eggplant or chicken parm, you have a soft, warm filling that gets sandwiched into a crusty, toasted hero roll, covered with a bit of mozzarella, and broiled until the cheese is toasted. The added sauce, cheese, and oven time refresh all of the qualities we love about lasagna straight out of the oven, and you get to stretch your leftovers out for a few more meals.

1 (8-inch-long) soft hero, sub, or grinder roll

1 square leftover lasagna (see Note)

½ cup Classic & Simple Red Sauce (page 130), warm

½ cup shredded low-moisture mozzarella cheese (not fresh)

1 tablespoon freshly grated Parmesan cheese

Dried red pepper flakes

1. **Pre-toast the hero:** Preheat the oven to 375°F with a rack in the upper third. Slice through the hero roll lengthwise and without slicing all the way through (it should open like a book). Transfer the roll to a foil-lined baking sheet, cut side up, and bake just until warm and slightly crusty, 2 to 3 minutes.

2. **Prep the sandwiches:** Cut the lasagna into ¾-inch-wide slices that are about as long as the hero roll. Add a small ladle of red sauce to each roll and arrange the lasagna strip over the sauce so the cut sides face the bun halves. Spoon another small ladle of sauce on top and sprinkle with the mozzarella and Parmesan.

3. **Bake the sandwiches:** Bake until bubbling and golden, about 15 minutes. Sprinkle with a pinch of crushed red pepper flakes. Close the sandwich and cut in half before serving.

NOTE

Any tomatoey lasagna works here such as:
- *Classic Meat Sauce & Ricotta Lasagna (page 28)*
- *Eggplant Parm Lasagna (page 53)*
- *Summer Veggie Lasagna (page 38)*
- *Slow-Cooker Spinach Ricotta Lasagna (page 40)*
- *Lasagna with Meatballs & Sunday Sauce (page 31)*
- *Ethiopian Lasagna (page 35)*
- *Porchetta-Spiced Pork Shoulder Lasagna (page 71)*

FRIED LASAGNA BITES

MAKES
45 BITES
(8 TO 10
SNACK-SIZE
SERVINGS)

These lasagna bites come from the genius of chef Mark Ladner. They are crispy on the outside, like the corner bits of a baked lasagna, and soft and gooey on the inside. They're not *that* difficult to make, but they do require getting started two days before you're planning to eat them, considering they need to be refrigerated, frozen, rested, and then frozen again. That said, because they are cooked from frozen, they can be made days before a party and fried right before serving. Think of them as a lasagnified version of the Pizza Rolls you used to keep in your dorm freezer. To simplify, you can skip the homemade marinara sauce (go straight to step 4) and use your favorite store-bought brand.

SPECIAL
EQUIPMENT
2 standard
half-sheet pans
(18 x 13-inch with
1-inch rim) or 2
(18 x 13-inch)
baking dishes;
cooling rack (18 x
13-inch or larger);
fry thermometer

Marinara Sauce

Extra-virgin olive oil

Coarse kosher salt
(preferably Diamond
Crystal)

½ teaspoon dried red
pepper flakes

2 medium garlic cloves,
peeled and smashed

½ small yellow onion, finely
chopped (about ¼ cup)

1 (28-ounce) can whole
peeled plum tomatoes
(preferably San Marzano)
with their juices

1½ tablespoons double-
concentrated tomato paste
(or 3 tablespoons regular
tomato paste)

½ loosely packed cup fresh
basil leaves

1 tablespoon sugar

Lasagna Bites

1 large egg, lightly beaten,
plus 1 large egg white

1½ cups fresh whole-milk
ricotta cheese

3 tablespoons freshly grated
Parmesan cheese

2 tablespoons freshly grated
Pecorino Romano cheese

Pinch of freshly grated
nutmeg

15 dry lasagna noodles,
cooked and cooled
(see page 16)

1 cup all-purpose flour

2 quarts (½ gallon)
canola oil, for frying

(recipe continues)

1. Make the marinara sauce: Add 1½ tablespoons olive oil, 1 teaspoon salt, the red pepper flakes, garlic, and onion to a small Dutch oven or medium saucepan set over medium heat. Cook, stirring often, until the garlic is very lightly golden and the onion is soft, about 3 minutes. Transfer the mixture to a food processor (set the pot aside to use again in step 3).

2. To the onion mixture, add the tomatoes with their juices, tomato paste, basil, sugar, and ½ teaspoon salt and puree until well blended but with pieces of tomato remaining.

3. Return the sauce to the Dutch oven, bring it to a gentle simmer over low heat, and cook until reduced by about half, about 1 hour (you should end up with approximately 2 to 2½ cups of sauce). Remove from the heat and let cool completely. (The sauce can be kept, covered and refrigerated, for up to 4 days, or frozen for up to 1 month.)

4. Make the ricotta filling: In a mixing bowl, combine the egg; the egg white; the ricotta, Parmesan, and Pecorino Romano cheeses; and the nutmeg. Using a rubber spatula, mix the ingredients well until the egg and the cheeses are fully combined. (The cheese filling can be kept, covered and refrigerated, for up to 3 days.)

5. Assemble the lasagna: Line the inside of a 13 x 18-inch rimmed baking sheet or baking dish with plastic wrap, making sure all of the edges of the pan are covered. Evenly spread 1 tablespoon olive oil and 2 tablespoons of the marinara sauce over the plastic wrap. Add a layer of noodles (about 3 noodles), laying them inside the baking sheet lengthwise, barely overlapping their edges so there is no space between the noodles. Spread 3 more tablespoons of marinara over the noodles, then use a large spoon to evenly spread out 5 tablespoons of the ricotta filling over the sauce. Lay a second layer of noodles over the top crosswise, trimming their lengths to fit the pan as you go. Repeat with another 3 tablespoons of the marinara and 5 tablespoons of the ricotta filling, and then add the third layer of noodles lengthwise. Repeat one more time so you have 4 layers of noodles (alternating lengthwise and crosswise), then end with a fifth layer of noodles followed by 1 tablespoon olive oil and 2 tablespoons of marinara spread evenly on top. (Any remaining sauce can be kept, covered and refrigerated, for up to 4 days, or frozen for up to 1 month.)

6. Wrap the top of the lasagna with plastic wrap, ensuring that the entire lasagna is completely sealed. Place a second 13 x 18-inch baking sheet on top of the lasagna and add 8 to 12 pounds of weight to the pan to compress the lasagna. (Cans of soda, a pot of water, or a small free weight will work well.) Refrigerate the lasagna overnight.

7. *Trim the lasagna into bites:* Remove the lasagna from the refrigerator. Remove the top baking sheet and the top layer of plastic wrap. Flip the lasagna over onto a large cutting board and remove the remaining plastic wrap. Using a sharp knife, trim about ¼ inch from all four sides of the lasagna, creating clean edges, and discard the scraps. Cut the lasagna into 1-inch squares (it's important that all the bites be about the same size when you fry them later).

8. Arrange the lasagna bites in a single layer on a wire rack set over a rimmed baking sheet (if the bites fall apart as you transfer them, press them back together with your fingers). Place the tray of lasagna bites in the freezer for at least 5 hours, or until they are frozen through and completely solid, up to overnight.

9. Remove the lasagna bites from the freezer. Add the flour to a large mixing bowl and toss the frozen bites in the flour to lightly coat them on all sides, shaking off any excess flour before returning them to the wire rack (reserve the bowl with the remaining flour). Let the bites stand on the rack at room temperature for 4 hours, until they thaw out completely and the flour is absorbed into the bites. Then return the tray of bites to the freezer for at least 5 more hours, or until they are frozen through and completely solid.

10. Remove the lasagna bites from the freezer. Working quickly, toss the frozen bites in the reserved flour until they are lightly coated again. Shake off any excess flour and return them to the freezer. (The bites should be durable at this point and can be stored in a plastic container or plastic bag for up to 5 days before frying.)

11. *Fry the lasagna bites:* Warm the remaining marinara sauce. Meanwhile, in a large pot, heat the canola oil over medium-high heat to 350°F. Fry the frozen lasagna bites 8 at a time until they puff up slightly and are golden brown, about 6½ minutes. Using a slotted spoon or tongs, transfer them to a wire rack to drain. Season with ½ teaspoon salt while hot. Repeat with the remaining bites, making sure the oil always returns to 350°F before adding the next batch. Whisk 1 tablespoon olive oil into the marinara sauce and serve it as a dipping sauce on the side.

3

OTHER BAKED PASTAS

Think for a moment about everything you love about lasagna: melty cheese, burnt edges, an entire bubbling meal baked efficiently into one heroic casserole. These qualities exist in many baked pastas, from baked ziti to plump ricotta-filled shells.

Sometimes this looks like orderly rows of stuffed manicotti with sauce ladled over the top. Other times these pastas have an element of carefree chaos, like a tangle of macaroni, bathed in béchamel.

In this chapter, we'll explore all of those peaks and valleys, finding the best chewy, sometimes crispy qualities of those shells, macaroni, ziti, and orecchiette. We'll even show you how to turn the box of spaghetti at the back of your cupboard into a crisp, round, awe-inspiring pie.

BAKED ZITI

There are types of hunger that can be quelled by sensible lentil soups or pragmatic farro salads. But there's another type of hunger: the kind that takes over when you've just finished helping a friend move into a fourth-floor walk-up apartment, or when you've just trekked home from work through a bomb cyclone; and it can only be quelled by digging a cartoonishly large serving spoon into a deep dish of baked ziti and stuffing your face with this classic of the carbohydrate canon. We like using the Classic & Simple Red Sauce on page 130 or the Sunday Sauce on page 134 for this recipe, but you can always fortify this by adding some small meatballs or crumbled Italian sausage to the mix.

1 teaspoon coarse kosher salt (preferably Diamond Crystal), plus more for the pot

1 pound ziti

15 ounces ricotta cheese (about 1¾ cups)

2 tablespoons chopped fresh flat-leaf parsley

¼ cup freshly grated Pecorino Romano cheese

¼ teaspoon freshly ground black pepper

4 cups Classic & Simple Red Sauce (page 130) or Sunday Sauce (page 134), warm

8 ounces low-moisture mozzarella cheese (not fresh), shredded (2 cups)

1. Preheat the oven to 375°F and position a rack in the center. Bring a large pot of salted water to a boil. Add the ziti and cook according to package instructions, stirring occasionally, until just al dente. Drain and return the ziti to the pot.

2. In a medium bowl, combine the ricotta, parsley, and half of the Pecorino Romano. Season to taste with the salt and pepper.

3. Add the sauce to the pasta and stir to combine. Pour half of the ziti into an

8 x 11-inch (2-quart) glass or ceramic baking dish (see Note). Dollop the ricotta mixture on top in large spoonfuls. Sprinkle with half of the mozzarella. Spoon the remaining ziti on top, spreading to an even layer, and top with the remaining mozzarella and Pecorino Romano.

1. Cover and bake for 15 minutes, then uncover and bake until bubbling and browned, about 15 minutes longer. Let rest for 10 minutes before serving.

NOTE
Making baked ziti in a slightly deeper dish creates bigger pockets of ricotta—it stays creamier and moister this way.

PASTITSIO

Right up there with moussaka, pastitsio is one of Greece's great casserole ambassadors to the world, packed with fragrant cinnamon and clove-spiced lamb. Unlike a lot of the other gloriously messy baked pastas in this book, when you assemble pastitsio, you lay down the ziti neatly in the pan, completely parallel to one another, in a series of long rows. As a result, when you cut into the finished product, the cross section is full of perfectly round little bubbles of pasta, ready to catch any stray bits of the fluffy, toasted béchamel on top.

2 tablespoons extra-virgin olive oil, plus more for the dish

1 medium yellow onion, finely chopped

2 large garlic cloves, finely chopped

2 pounds ground lamb or beef (85% lean)

Coarse kosher salt (preferably Diamond Crystal) and freshly ground black pepper

2 teaspoons dried oregano (preferably Greek), crumbled

1½ teaspoons ground cinnamon

¼ teaspoon freshly grated nutmeg

Pinch of ground cloves or allspice

⅓ cup tomato paste

1 teaspoon sugar

1 pound Greek-style long ziti or Italian ziti

¾ cup freshly grated Kefalotyri or other salty, hard sheep's-milk cheese like Pecorino Romano

1 recipe (4 cups) Thick Béchamel (page 139)

2 large eggs

1. Preheat the oven to 375° with a rack in the lower third. Lightly oil a 9 x 13-inch (3-quart) glass or ceramic baking dish, preferably 3 inches deep.

2. Heat the oil in a large, deep skillet until shimmering. Add the onion and cook over medium-high heat, stirring occasionally, until translucent, about 5 minutes. Add the garlic and cook for 1 minute. Add the lamb and a generous pinch of salt and pepper and cook, breaking it into small pieces, until all of the liquid is evaporated and the lamb is sizzling and beginning to brown, 8 to 10 minutes.

3. Add the oregano, cinnamon, nutmeg, and cloves and cook, stirring, for 1 minute. Stir in the tomato paste and cook, stirring, until it darkens slightly, 1 to 2 minutes. Add 3 cups water and the sugar and bring to a boil, scraping up any bits stuck to the pan. Simmer over medium heat until thickened and reduced slightly, 15 to 20 minutes. Season generously with salt and pepper.

4. Meanwhile, bring a large pot of salted water to a boil. Add the pasta and cook until barely al dente, 5 to 8 minutes. Drain and rinse under cold water. Drain again, then arrange half of the noodles in the same ● ● ● ● ●

direction in the prepared baking dish. Spoon all of the meat sauce evenly over the noodles, then top with the remaining noodles, arranging them in the same direction.

5. Stir ½ cup of the Kefalotyri into the béchamel. Spoon 1 cup into a bowl and whisk in the eggs. Whisk the egg mixture back into the remaining béchamel and spoon over the noodles in an even layer. Sprinkle the remaining cheese on top. Bake until bubbling and the top is lightly golden, 35 to 40 minutes. Remove from the oven. Let rest for 15 minutes before serving.

LASAGNA TIMPANO

If you've ever seen the movie *Big Night*, you'll remember the frenzied dance of Stanley Tucci and Tony Shalhoub kneading and rolling out pasta dough, ladling sauce, and scooping meatballs and boiled eggs into a metal pan shaped like a timpani drum–hence the name. After baking the pasta-filled creation, the men's four hands rotate the overturned pan cautiously, then lift it with bated breath to reveal the pristine wheel of baked pasta within. Our slightly more diminutive (yet still gasp-inducing) extra-deep-dish version skips the meatballs and eggs in favor of Italian sausage and ground beef, but it will still make a convincing prop for all of your Stanley Tucci cosplay dinner parties.

1 tablespoon extra-virgin olive oil

1 medium yellow onion, finely chopped

2 large garlic cloves, finely chopped

1 pound lean ground beef (93% lean)

2 teaspoons coarse kosher salt (preferably Diamond Crystal)

1 teaspoon freshly ground black pepper

⅓ cup tomato paste

1 teaspoon dried oregano, crumbled

1 teaspoon sugar

12 ounces sweet or hot Italian link sausage

1 pound ricotta cheese

½ pound low-moisture mozzarella (not fresh), coarsely grated

2 tablespoons chopped fresh flat-leaf parsley

¼ cup plus 2 tablespoons freshly grated Parmesan cheese

2 large eggs

2 tablespoons unsalted butter, melted, plus more for the pie plate

2 tablespoons plain dry bread crumbs

1 recipe (12 sheets; 16 ounces) Fresh Pasta Sheets (page 129), cooked

Classic & Simple Red Sauce (page 130), warm, for serving

NOTE
If you don't have an extra-deep 10-inch pie plate, you can use a 3-quart enameled cast-iron casserole or Dutch oven; a 9 x 3-inch-deep cake pan; a 3-quart soufflé dish; a 3-quart stainless bowl; or a large, deep ovenproof skillet.

1. Cook the meat: Preheat the oven to 375°F with a rack in the center. Heat the oil in a large, deep skillet over medium-high heat until shimmering, about 2 minutes. Add the onion and cook over medium-high heat, stirring occasionally, until translucent, about 5 minutes. Add the garlic and cook for 1 minute. Add the beef, ½ teaspoon of the salt, and ¼ teaspoon of the pepper and cook, breaking the meat into small pieces with a wooden spoon, until all of the liquid is evaporated and the beef is sizzling and beginning to brown, 8 to 10 minutes. If after browning there is a lot of fat in the pan, spoon the mixture into a strainer to remove as much fat as possible, then return the meat to the pan.

(recipe continues)

*2. **Make the sauce:*** Add in the tomato paste and cook, stirring, until it darkens slightly, 1 to 2 minutes. Add 2 cups water, the oregano, and the sugar and bring to a boil, scraping up any bits stuck to the pan. Lower the heat to medium and simmer until the mixture is very thick and reduced to 2½ cups, 15 to 20 minutes. Season with another ½ teaspoon of the salt and ¼ teaspoon of the pepper.

3. Meanwhile, prick the sausages all over with a fork. Heat a medium skillet over medium-high heat. Add the sausages, cover, and cook, turning occasionally, until browned all over and firm to the touch, 8 to 10 minutes. Transfer to a cutting board and slice lengthwise in half.

*4. **Make the cheese mixture:*** In a medium bowl, combine the ricotta, mozzarella, parsley, and the ¼ cup of Parmesan. Season with the remaining 1 teaspoon of salt and ½ teaspoon of pepper. Add the eggs and stir to combine.

5. Brush a 10-inch, extra-deep pie plate with some of the butter (see Note, page 93). Cut a circle of parchment paper to fit the bottom and brush it with butter. In a small bowl, combine the bread crumbs and the remaining 2 tablespoons of Parmesan. Add the mixture to the pan and turn to coat the sides and bottom completely. Tap out the excess and reserve.

*6. **Assemble the timpano:*** Arrange a layer of 3 or 4 noodles in the pan, overlapping and extending 2 inches over the sides. Spread half of the meat sauce across the bottom. Cut a few noodles to fit the dish and arrange a layer over the meat sauce. Top with the ricotta mixture, spreading to the edges. Tuck the sausages into the ricotta to submerge and top with another layer of noodles, cut to fit. Top with the remaining meat sauce. Fold in the overhanging noodles. Cover with a final layer of noodles, cut to fit, and brush generously with melted butter. Sprinkle with the reserved Parmesan bread crumbs. Butter a circle of parchment to place buttered side down onto the lasagna.

*7. **Bake the timpano:*** Cover the pan tightly with foil and bake for 60 minutes. Uncover and bake until the top and sides are golden and sizzling, 15 to 20 minutes longer. Let rest in the pan for at least 1 hour, or preferably 2 hours, until set.

8. Place a large, flat plate over the timpano. Using both hands and oven mitts, grab the pie dish and plate together and carefully flip so the plate is on the bottom. Give the plate a gentle rap on the table to loosen and remove the pie dish. Peel off the parchment. Cut the timpano into wedges and serve with the red sauce.

SPINACH MANICOTTI *with* CREAMY TOMATO SAUCE

Manicotti might have the same core elements as a baked ziti or ravioli, but there's a certain formality to its tidy presentation, especially when you're talking about traditional Italian manicotti made with crepes instead of boiled and stuffed pasta. The *crespelle* (as a *nonna* might say) are wrapped lovingly around a filling and then baked in a single layer across the bottom of a baking dish. In addition to being a little easier to fill than slippery parboiled pasta, the crepes have a soft sponginess that can soak up a creamy sauce. Here, oven-roasted garlic becomes the sweet flavoring in a spinach-ricotta filling, and the stuffed manicotti are covered in a cream-spiked tomato sauce before baking.

1 head of garlic, separated into cloves (not peeled)

6 fresh thyme sprigs

Extra-virgin olive oil, for drizzling

4 tablespoons (½ stick) unsalted butter

2 shallots, chopped (about ½ cup)

¼ cup tomato paste

1 (28-ounce) can whole peeled Italian tomatoes with their juices

Coarse kosher salt (preferably Diamond Crystal) and freshly ground black pepper

½ cup heavy cream

10 ounces frozen spinach, thawed and squeezed dry

1½ pounds ricotta cheese (3 cups)

½ cup freshly grated Parmesan cheese

2 large eggs

16 Crespelle (page 137)

1. Preheat the oven to 375°F with a rack in the center. Place the unpeeled garlic cloves and the thyme sprigs in the center of a square sheet of foil. Drizzle with 1 tablespoon oil. Fold up and seal the edges to create a packet and roast until the garlic is tender, about 30 minutes.

2. While the garlic roasts, make the sauce: Melt the butter in a medium pot over medium-high heat. Add the shallots and cook, stirring, until golden, about 4 minutes. Stir in the tomato paste and cook, stirring, until it

darkens slightly, 1 to 2 minutes. Add the tomatoes and 4 cups water, then season with 1 teaspoon salt and ¼ teaspoon pepper and bring to a boil, crushing the tomatoes with a potato masher or wooden spoon. Simmer, partially covered, on medium-low heat until reduced to about 4 cups, 30 to 35 minutes.

3. Stir the cream into the sauce and, using an immersion blender or regular blender, puree until smooth. Season to taste with salt and pepper.

(recipe continues)

4. To make the filling, squeeze the roasted garlic from their skins into a medium bowl and mash to a paste. Pull the crisp thyme leaves from the stems and add them to the bowl (discard the stems). Add the spinach, ricotta, and ¼ cup of the Parmesan and season with 2 teaspoons salt and ½ teaspoon pepper. Add the eggs and stir until combined.

5. Spread ¾ cup of the sauce in the bottom of a 9 x 13-inch (3-quart) glass or ceramic baking dish. Arrange a *crespella* on a work surface, browned side down. Add about ¼ cup of the filling, spreading it in a line down the center of the *crespella*. Roll into a cylinder (with open ends) and place the manicotti in the baking dish, seam side down. Repeat with the remaining *crespelle* and filling. Cover with 1½ cups of the sauce (save the rest for serving). Sprinkle with the remaining Parmesan and bake until bubbling and lightly browned, about 30 minutes. Let rest for 15 minutes before serving with the remaining sauce.

CHEESY SKILLET BAKED SPAGHETTI

When we think of baked pasta, we tend to think of the stuffed shells (page 103) and baked zitis (page 89) of the world. But baked spaghetti (also called spaghetti pie) plays up a lot of spaghetti's best qualities. Here, sauce and sausage get evenly distributed throughout the dish, and the skinny noodles toast up to form hundreds of little crispy bits on top. But the best part about this simple recipe? All of the cooking goes down in one skillet. You brown some sausage, build the tomato sauce, and cook the spaghetti *right in the sauce*, then sprinkle some cheese on top and bake the whole thing. The result is a pie that's crispy on top and full of saucy swirls.

2 tablespoons extra-virgin olive oil

8 ounces lean ground beef (85% lean) or bulk sweet Italian sausage

3 large garlic cloves, finely chopped

1 small yellow onion, finely chopped

1 teaspoon chopped fresh rosemary

¼ to ½ teaspoon dried red pepper flakes

2 tablespoons tomato paste

1 (28-ounce) can whole peeled Italian tomatoes, chopped in their can with kitchen scissors

1 tablespoon coarse kosher salt (preferably Diamond Crystal)

1 pound dried spaghetti (uncooked), broken in half

¼ cup plus 2 tablespoons freshly grated Pecorino Romano cheese

8 ounces low-moisture mozzarella cheese (not fresh), shredded

1. Preheat the oven to 425°F with a rack in the upper third. Heat the oil in a 14-inch ovenproof skillet over medium-high heat until shimmering, about 2 minutes. Add the ground beef and cook, breaking up large pieces with a spoon, until browned, about 5 minutes. Add the garlic, onion, rosemary, and red pepper flakes and cook, stirring occasionally, until the onion is translucent, about 5 minutes. Stir in the tomato paste and cook, stirring, until it darkens slightly, 1 to 2 minutes.

2. Stir in the canned tomatoes and their juices, 5 cups water, and the salt. Cover and bring to a boil. Add the spaghetti and, using a wooden spoon, turn and stir the spaghetti in the liquid until it begins to soften, about 5 minutes. Reduce the heat to a simmer and continue to cook, stirring frequently, until the pasta is al dente, about 11 minutes. Stir up from the bottom and sides of the skillet to ensure the pasta cooks evenly and doesn't stick to the pan.

3. Remove the skillet from the heat and stir in the Pecorino Romano cheese. Sprinkle the mozzarella on top, transfer the skillet to the oven, and bake until bubbling and the cheese is melted and browned in spots, about 12 minutes. Let sit for 5 minutes before serving.

CREAMY TOMATO BAKED ORECCHIETTE *with* SAUSAGE & CHEESE

In the realm of baked pastas, orecchiette is an underrated, though brilliant, shape to cook with. Why? Because the "little ears" have a way of hugging themselves around whatever you mix with it–in this case little browned bits of Italian sausage and pockets of soft ricotta. The creamy tomato sauce makes this dish a little bit reminiscent of penne alla vodka, but baked in a deep Dutch oven to keep everything moist and creamy, with a top layer of melted mozzarella.

1 tablespoon extra-virgin olive oil

1 pound sweet or hot Italian sausage, casings removed

3 large garlic cloves, finely chopped

1 tablespoon fresh thyme leaves

½ cup tomato paste

1 cup heavy cream

3 cups chicken broth

Coarse kosher salt (preferably Diamond Crystal) and freshly ground black pepper

1 pound ricotta cheese

¼ cup freshly grated Parmesan cheese

8 ounces low-moisture mozzarella cheese (not fresh), shredded (2 cups)

1 pound orecchiette

1. Heat the oil in a medium enameled lidded cast-iron casserole or Dutch oven (3 to 5 quarts; the deeper the pot, the creamier and moister the finished pasta) over medium-high heat until shimmering, about 2 minutes. Add the sausage and cook, breaking it into bite-size pieces with a wooden spoon, until lightly browned and cooked through, 8 to 10 minutes. Add the garlic and thyme and cook over medium heat until fragrant, about 1 minute. Stir in the tomato paste and cook, stirring, until it darkens slightly, 1 to 2 minutes. Add the cream and chicken broth and bring to a boil. Season lightly with a few pinches of salt and pepper. Simmer, partially covered, on medium-low heat until reduced slightly, 20 to 25 minutes.

2. In a medium bowl, combine the ricotta, half of the Parmesan, and half of the mozzarella. Season to taste with salt and pepper.

3. Meanwhile, preheat the oven to 375°F with a rack in the center and bring a large pot of salted water to a boil. Add the orecchiette to the boiling water and cook, stirring occasionally, until al dente, 8 to 11 minutes. Drain and return to the pasta pot. Add the sauce and stir to combine. Season to taste with salt and pepper.

4. Return half of the pasta to the casserole and spread in an even layer. Dollop the ricotta mixture on top, followed by the remaining pasta. Sprinkle with the remaining mozzarella and Parmesan. Cover with the lid and bake for 15 minutes, then uncover and bake until bubbling and browned, about 25 minutes longer. Let rest for 10 minutes before serving.

ROTISSERIE CHICKEN TETRAZZINI

Tetrazzini is a dish that you might associate with *Maury* (that would be the TV show hosted by Sir Povich, a classic episode when a man named Paul left his girlfriend for a woman who made outstanding chicken tetrazzini) and some of the early twentieth century's most dismal casseroles full of cream of mushroom soup. This revamped version takes all of its best attributes (creamy pasta and buttery cracker-crumb topping) and updates them with shredded rotisserie chicken, Parmesan, and fresh mushrooms that are browned in butter and sweetened with shallots. Paul loves it!

Coarse kosher salt (preferably Diamond Crystal)

2 tablespoons unsalted butter, plus more for the dish

1 pound white button mushrooms, sliced

¼ cup chopped shallots

1 tablespoon fresh thyme leaves

¼ teaspoon cayenne pepper

Freshly ground black pepper

½ cup dry white wine (or chicken broth)

1½ pounds (4 cups) shredded rotisserie chicken (from 1 chicken, skin removed, juices reserved)

8 ounces cream cheese, at room temperature

1 (5-ounce) package frozen baby peas

1 pound linguine (not thin or fini linguine)

1 recipe (4 cups) Classic Béchamel (page 139), warm

1½ cups freshly grated Parmesan cheese

1 cup crushed Ritz crackers (1 sleeve)

1. Bring a large pot of salted water to a boil. Preheat the oven to 375°F and position a rack in the lower third. Butter a 9 x 13-inch (3-quart) glass or ceramic baking dish.

2. Meanwhile, melt the 2 tablespoons butter in a large skillet over medium-high heat. Add the mushrooms and cook until any liquid is evaporated and the mushrooms are lightly browned, about 10 minutes. Add the shallots, thyme, and cayenne, season with salt and black pepper, and cook until the shallots are translucent, 2 to 3 minutes. Add the wine and any accumulated juices from the rotisserie chicken and bring to a boil, scraping up any browned bits stuck to the pan with a wooden spoon. Cook until the liquid is evaporated,

about 5 minutes. Remove the skillet from the heat and stir in the cream cheese until melted, then the chicken and peas.

3. Break the linguine in half, then add it to the boiling water and cook, stirring occasionally, until al dente, 8 to 11 minutes. Reserve ½ cup of the pasta cooking water, then drain the linguine and return it to the pot. Add the béchamel, Parmesan, and chicken–mushroom mixture to the linguine in the pot and stir to combine. Add the reserved pasta water, a few tablespoons at a time, to thin the sauce slightly. Season generously with salt and black pepper and transfer to the baking dish. Scatter the cracker crumbs on top and bake until golden and bubbling, 20 to 30 minutes. Serve.

ROASTED POBLANO PEPPER-STUFFED SHELLS

There's something irresistibly heartwarming about the way shell pasta hugs whatever's nearby, whether it's the peas that fit perfectly into mini shells or the ricotta and sauce that you use to inflate a batch of jumbo shells before baking. For these slightly spicy stuffed shells, we use a filling of ricotta flavored with roasted poblano chile peppers and shredded mozzarella, but you can swap in any of the other flavored ricottas on page 136 if you prefer. The filling gets piped into the shells out of a resealable plastic bag, and the shell shape helps it stay put even as the filling softens and melts in the oven. This recipe uses up a whole box of jumbo shells, distributed across two baking dishes. You can eat one tonight and save the other in the freezer for later, but you can also easily cut this recipe in half.

Coarse kosher salt (preferably Diamond Crystal), for the pot

1 pound jumbo shells

1 recipe Roasted Poblano Pepper Ricotta (or other flavored ricotta cheese; see page 136)

1 pound low-moisture mozzarella cheese (not fresh), shredded

1 recipe (4½ cups) Classic & Simple Red Sauce (page 130), warm

½ cup freshly grated Pecorino Romano cheese

1. Preheat the oven to 375°F with a rack in the center. Bring a large pot of salted water to a boil. Add the shells and cook, gently stirring occasionally, until just al dente, about 8 minutes. Drain and rinse with cool water.

2. Meanwhile, combine the roasted poblano pepper ricotta with half of the mozzarella. Transfer the filling to a resealable plastic bag and press to seal. Using scissors, snip a corner of the bag so the opening is ½ inch wide.

3. Hold 1 shell in your hand and squeeze gently to widen the opening. With your other hand, hold the bag, position the tip in the shell, and squeeze gently to fill, taking care not to overfill. Set the shells on a work surface and repeat with the remaining pasta and filling. Add any remaining cheese mixture to any less-filled shells, so they are all more or less evenly filled.

4. Spoon ¾ cup of the sauce into each of two medium 1½- to 2-quart glass or ceramic baking dishes. Arrange the stuffed shells in the dishes, open side up, and top each dish with 1½ cups sauce. Sprinkle the Pecorino Romano and remaining mozzarella on top and cover with foil. Bake for 30 minutes, then uncover and bake until lightly bubbling and browned in spots, 15 to 20 minutes. Let the shells sit for 15 minutes before serving.

MORE IS MORE TRIPLE CHEESE MAC & CHEESE

There's a time and a place for moderation. This is not one of those times. When it comes to mac and cheese, more is more. Nobody ever *kind of* wants mac and cheese–it's a "go big or go home" situation. More creamy béchamel; more toasty, buttery, crunchy topping; and most obviously, more cheese. For this mac, we called in a dream team of Cheddar, Colby-Jack, and Parmesan, and we're quadrupling down on the cheese by forgoing the quaint bread-crumb topping in favor of crushed Cheez-Its crackers.

Unsalted butter, for the dish

1 pound sharp Cheddar cheese, cut into ½-inch cubes (about 4 cups)

8 ounces Colby-Jack cheese, cut into ½-inch cubes (or American cheese from the deli counter; about 2 cups)

1 recipe (4 cups) Classic Béchamel (page 139), warm

1 tablespoon Dijon mustard

Coarse kosher salt (preferably Diamond Crystal)

¼ teaspoon freshly ground black pepper

1 pound elbow macaroni

¼ cup freshly grated Parmesan cheese

1 cup lightly crushed cheese crackers, such as Cheez-Its or Goldfish

Preheat the oven to 350°F and generously butter a 9 x 13-inch (3-quart) glass or ceramic baking dish. Add half of the Cheddar and Colby-Jack to the béchamel and cook over low heat, stirring, until the cheeses are melted. Turn off the heat and stir in the mustard, 1 teaspoon salt, and the pepper.

1. Meanwhile, bring a large pot of salted water to a boil. Add the macaroni and cook, stirring frequently, until barely al dente, 3 to 4 minutes. Drain well, shaking out any excess water. Return the pasta to the pot and remove from the heat. Add the cheese sauce and the remaining cubed Cheddar and Colby-Jack and stir until evenly combined but not melted. Pour the mixture into the prepared dish, spreading it into an even layer.

2. In a small bowl, combine the Parmesan and cracker crumbs and sprinkle over the macaroni. Bake until bubbling and golden, 40 to 45 minutes. Let rest for 15 minutes before serving.

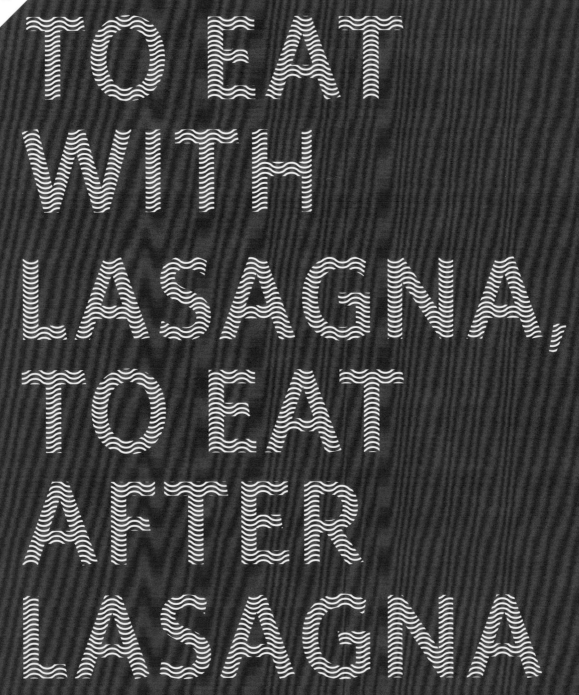

4

TO EAT
WITH
LASAGNA,
TO EAT
AFTER
LASAGNA

When you find a good neighborhood Italian

restaurant you love, it's the bells and whistles like warm garlic bread and crunchy iceberg lettuce that make the whole experience so comforting and inviting. This chapter will help you channel that feeling at home. There will be Parmesan croutons. There will be caramel *budino* and even melted Nutella baked into a lasagna that's topped with a layer of toasted marshmallow. And there is tiramisu, of course.

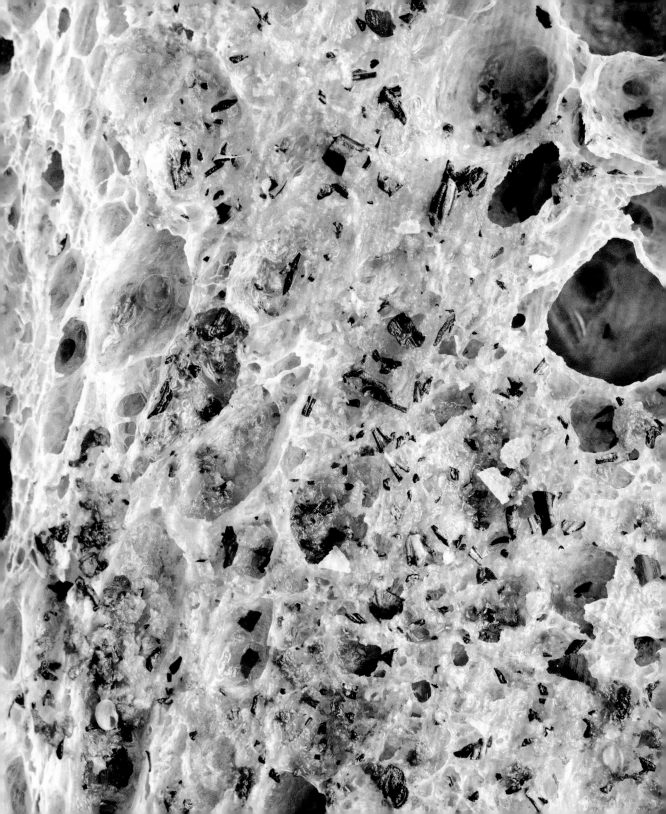

VERY GOOD GARLIC BREAD

TO EAT WITH
LASAGNA, TO EAT
AFTER LASAGNA

MAKES
1 LOAF

Like Fudgie the Whale ice cream cakes from Carvel, or calling in sick to work so you can go to the beach, garlic bread is one of those things you forget about until you need an infallible way to cheer someone (or yourself) up. There are no obscure ingredients to source, and there are no surprises when you make it. The secret is lots of butter and lots of garlic. Simple. If you're in a fancy mood, you can throw in some smoked paprika, cracked fennel seeds, or fresh sage. Even if you stick to the classic, your home will smell better than it has in months.

5 large garlic cloves, finely chopped

1 tablespoon finely chopped fresh rosemary

4 tablespoons (½ stick) unsalted butter

¼ cup extra-virgin olive oil

Pinch of dried red pepper flakes (optional)

1 loaf (12 to 16 ounces) Italian bread or ciabatta, split lengthwise

¼ teaspoon flaky sea salt (like Maldon or Jacobsen)

1. Preheat the oven to 375°F and position a rack in the center. On a cutting board, chop the garlic and rosemary together. Melt the butter in the olive oil in a small skillet over high heat. Add the garlic–rosemary mixture and red pepper flakes, if using, and cook until fragrant but not browned, about 1 minute. Immediately brush the mixture over the cut surfaces of the bread, spreading it to the edges.

2. Close the loaf, transfer to a baking sheet, and bake until crisp, flipping once, about 6 minutes. Open the loaf so the cut sides are facing up and turn on the broiler. Broil just until golden and sizzling, 1 to 2 minutes. (Watch carefully as ovens vary greatly— nothing is sadder than burnt garlic bread). Sprinkle with the flaky salt and serve.

ITALIAN RESTAURANT ICEBERG LETTUCE SALAD

Never trust anyone who tells you they don't eat iceberg lettuce. These poor green globes have gotten a bad rap for decades as nutrition-less, flavorless second fiddles to the kales and arugulas of the world. But no other lettuce can beat its crunch, its refreshing contrast to creamy dressings and spicy peperoncini–or its steadfast integrity in the face of wilty conditions. This spin on a classic Italian-American salad capitalizes on all of those attributes, pairing the iceberg with Sicilian green olives, red onion, cherry tomatoes, and a knockout garlicky, creamy dressing you last tasted on Taylor Street or Arthur Avenue. If you have leftovers, consider tucking them into a Leftover Lasagna Parm Sandwich (page 81) once it's out of the oven.

1 large garlic clove, smashed

Coarse kosher salt
(preferably Diamond Crystal)

2 tablespoons mayonnaise

2 tablespoons red wine
vinegar

½ teaspoon dried oregano

1 teaspoon sugar

¼ cup plus 2 tablespoons
blended oil (3 tablespoons
olive oil and 3 tablespoons
vegetable oil)

Pinch of freshly ground
black pepper

1 head of iceberg lettuce,
cored and coarsely chopped

1 inner celery rib,
thinly sliced

½ small red onion,
thinly sliced

½ cup cherry tomatoes,
halved

¼ cup cracked Sicilian
green olives, pitted

8 peperoncini

2 ounces Parmesan cheese,
shaved with a vegetable
peeler (1 cup)

1. In a large bowl, using a fork, mash the garlic with a generous pinch of salt to form a paste. Whisk in the mayonnaise, vinegar, oregano, and sugar. While whisking, slowly drizzle in the oil, whisking until the dressing is emulsified. Season to taste with salt and pepper.

2. Add the lettuce, celery, onion, cherry tomatoes, olives, peperoncini, and Parmesan and toss to combine. Serve right away.

HUILE D'OLIVE
EXTRA VIERGE

EXTRA VIRGIN
OLIVE OIL

OLIO EXTRA VERGINE DI OLIVA

PREMIÈRE QUALITÉ   Ⓤ

3 LITERS   101 FL OZ
100% PRODUIT D'ITALIE

OLIO EXTRA VERGINE DI OLIVA

PREMIUM SELECT   Ⓤ

3 LITERS   101 FL OZ
100% PRODUCT OF ITALY

SICILIAN
EXTRA VIRG
OLIVE OI

101 FL OZ (3 QT 5 FL OZ) 3 LI

SINCE 1916
Partan
BRAN

ASARO
PARTANNA

FIRST COLD
PRESSED

EXTRA VIRGIN
Olive Oil

OLIO EXTRA VERGINE DI OLIVA

PREMIUM SELECT   Ⓤ

101 FL OZ (3 QT 5 FL OZ) 3 LITERS
IMPORTED FROM ITALY

EXTRA VIRGIN
Olive Oil

OLIO EXTRA VERGINE DI OLIVA

PREMIUM SELECT   Ⓤ

101 FL OZ (3 QT 5 FL OZ) 3 LITERS
IMPORTED FROM ITALY

SICILI
EXTRA V
OLIVE

101 FL OZ (3 QT 5 FL

SINCE 1
Parta
BRA

ASAR
PARTAN

CAESAR SALAD
with PARMESAN CROUTONS

Caesar salad makes an ideal counterpunch to lasagna, less because it involves fresh vegetables (although, sure, there's some lettuce involved) and more because the zap of raw garlic, briny anchovy, and acidic lemon juice cuts through lasagna's saucy, carb-y richness like a sharp knife through a stick of butter. This salad, topped with Parmesan croutons, holds its own even without lasagna. It would make a great dinner with a loaf of Very Good Garlic Bread (page 109) or a batch of Why Knot Garlic Knots (page 114), or you could add a little grilled steak or chicken and call it a day.

½ loaf (6-inch length) of Italian bread, sliced ½ inch thick

½ cup blended oil (¼ cup olive oil and ¼ cup vegetable oil)

Coarse kosher salt (preferably Diamond Crystal) and freshly ground black pepper

¼ cup plus 2 tablespoons freshly grated Parmesan cheese

1 large garlic clove

2 large anchovy fillets, chopped (or ½ tablespoon anchovy paste)

2 tablespoons mayonnaise

2 tablespoons fresh lemon juice

1 pound (2 large heads) romaine lettuce, cored, ends trimmed, and leaves torn into bite-size pieces

1. Preheat the oven to 375°F. Tear the bread slices into 1-inch pieces and toss them in a medium bowl with 2 tablespoons of the oil. Season with salt and pepper and spread them on a rimmed baking sheet. Toast the bread, tossing once or twice, until lightly browned and crisp on the outside, about 10 minutes. Return the croutons to the bowl and toss with 2 tablespoons of the Parmesan. Spread the croutons on the baking sheet and bake again, just until the cheese is melted and nutty, about 5 minutes longer. Let cool.

2. Meanwhile, on a cutting board, use the side of a chef's knife to chop and mash the garlic clove and anchovies to a paste. Transfer to a salad bowl and whisk in the mayonnaise and lemon juice. Slowly whisk in the remaining ¼ cup plus 2 tablespoons of oil and season generously with pepper. Whisk in the remaining Parmesan and season with salt.

3. Add the lettuce to the dressing. Add the croutons and toss. Season with salt and pepper and serve right away.

WHY KNOT GARLIC KNOTS

Whether you're hungrily waiting for dinner to be served at your friend's kid's birthday party or you've just eaten three slices alone at the pizza parlor after work, nobody is ever disappointed to see a plate of garlic knots emerge from the kitchen, shining with warm butter and vibrating with a pleasantly potent garlic funk. Serving garlic knots at a dinner party is a vastly more exciting option than sliced bread or dinner rolls, and you can get them ready ahead of time, letting them proof on the baking sheet while you dole out Negronis and hellos. They can even be their own dinner, dipped in some Classic & Simple Red Sauce (page 130) and served with a salad. Just make sure you don't skimp on the garlic.

Dough

1½ teaspoons active dry yeast

1 cup lukewarm water (80°F to 90°F)

Pinch of sugar

2 cups all-purpose flour, plus more for kneading and rolling

1½ teaspoons kosher salt (preferably Diamond Crystal)

Extra-virgin olive oil

Topping

3 tablespoons unsalted butter

3 tablespoons extra-virgin olive oil

2 tablespoons finely chopped garlic

2 tablespoons finely chopped fresh flat-leaf parsley

Flaky sea salt (like Maldon or Jacobsen), to taste

MORE GARLIC KNOT TOPPINGS
Add these to the butter and oil in step 4:

• *Garlic, rosemary, and lemon zest*

• *Garlic, dried red pepper flakes, and dried oregano*

• *Garlic and fresh chopped chives*

1. Make the dough: In a large bowl, mix the yeast with ¼ cup of the warm water and the sugar and let stand until foamy, about 5 minutes. Add the remaining ¾ cup of warm water, the 2 cups of flour, and the kosher salt and stir to form a soft dough. Turn the dough out onto a well-floured work surface and knead, adding flour as necessary, until a silky but soft dough forms. Use a pastry scraper to help knead the dough. Transfer the dough to a lightly oiled bowl and brush all over with olive oil. Cover the bowl with plastic wrap and set aside until the dough has doubled in volume, about 1 hour.

2. Line 2 large baking sheets with parchment paper. Turn the dough onto a floured surface and gently press to deflate. Press or roll to a 6 x 10-inch rectangle. Cut the dough crosswise into 24 (½-inch-wide) strips, then gently tie the strips into knots and transfer to the baking sheets. Brush with oil, cover loosely with plastic, and let sit until risen and puffy, 30 minutes to 1 hour. Rinse and dry the bowl.

3. Bake the knots: Preheat the oven to 425°F and set racks in the lower and upper third positions. Bake the knots until golden, about 18 minutes, turning the pans once from front to back and shifting from top to bottom for even browning.

4. Meanwhile, make the topping:
In a small skillet, melt the butter in the oil on medium heat. When the foam subsides, add the garlic and cook, stirring, until fragrant but not browned, about 2 minutes. Stir in the parsley and transfer to a large bowl. When the knots are cooked, add them to the bowl and toss to coat evenly in the garlic butter. Sprinkle with flaky salt and transfer to a plate. Sprinkle with more flaky salt (or with one of the optional toppings; see opposite) and serve right away.

SWEET CRESPELLE *with* LEMON & TART CHERRY SAUCE

Crespelle, the Italian version of crepes, are traditionally used as wrappers for savory baked cannelloni and manicotti dishes (like the one on page 95). But by swapping in some butter for the olive oil and adding a tiny bit of sugar, the blintz-like pancakes become a great base for a dessert (or sweet breakfast). These are filled with a sweetened lemony mixture of farmer cheese (a mild, slightly denser version of cottage cheese), cream cheese, and egg, which gets melty and a little bit fluffy in the oven. You can top them with our tart cherry syrup recipe and a dusting of confectioners' sugar, along with fresh fruit; or try that jar of fancy jam someone gave you as a gift last summer that you never opened.

3 tablespoons unsalted butter, melted, plus more for the dish

15 ounces farmer cheese

8 ounces cream cheese, at room temperature

1 large egg plus 1 large egg yolk

¼ cup plus 3½ tablespoons granulated sugar

1 teaspoon pure vanilla extract

1 teaspoon grated lemon zest

Pinch of coarse kosher salt (preferably Diamond Crystal)

16 to 20 sweet Crespelle (see Note, page 137),

12 ounces tart cherry preserves

2 tablespoons fresh lemon juice

2 tablespoons kirsch (or other fruit brandy, such as Framboise or Mirabelle)

Confectioners' sugar, for dusting

Fresh berries, for serving

1. Preheat the oven to 375°F with a rack in the center. Generously butter a 9 x 13-inch (3-quart) glass or ceramic baking dish.

2. In a medium bowl, combine the farmer cheese, cream cheese, egg, egg yolk, ¼ cup plus 2 tablespoons of the granulated sugar, the vanilla, lemon zest, and salt and stir until smooth.

3. Arrange a *crespella* on a clean work surface, browned side up, and add a spoonful of the cheese filling to the center of each one. Fold up the bottom half of the *crespella,* covering the filling, then fold in both sides. Finally, fold the top over like an envelope and set the *crespella* in the baking dish, seam side

down. Continue with the remaining *crespelle* and filling, forming the blintzes, adding them to the baking dish in 2 neat rows, overlapping slightly.

4. Brush the tops of the rolls with the melted butter and sprinkle with the remaining 1½ tablespoons of granulated sugar. Bake until golden, about 35 minutes.

5. Meanwhile, in a small saucepan, combine the cherry preserves, lemon juice, kirsch, and ¼ cup water. Bring to a boil and cook for 2 minutes to boil off the alcohol. Serve the blintzes dusted with confectioners' sugar and drizzled with the sauce, and spoon fresh berries alongside.

~~~~~~

VARIATION
Sweet Crespelle Lasagna

To build the *crespelle* into a lasagna, generously butter a 9 x 13-inch (3-quart) baking dish and line it with 6 or 7 of the *crespelle,* overlapping and extending them 2 inches over the edges (completely covering the bottom and sides). Spread half of the cheese filling in an even layer, followed by 2 or 3 *crespelle,* just to cover the filling. Repeat with the remaining cheese filling and 2 or 3 more *crespelle.* Fold over the sides and top with the remaining *crespelle.* Brush with the butter and sprinkle with the remaining 1½ tablespoons of granulated sugar. Bake until golden, about 35 minutes. Set aside to rest for 5 to 10 minutes before slicing and serving.

TIRAMISU FOR THE 21ST CENTURY

TO EAT WITH
LASAGNA, TO EAT
AFTER LASAGNA

8 TO 12
SERVINGS

As much as we tend to think of tiramisu as one of the most iconic Italian desserts around, this dish really only started popping up on American restaurant menus in the 1980s. (If cannoli is the Dean Martin of Italian desserts, think of tiramisu as the Jon Bon Jovi.) But this doesn't prohibit it from being the hit of dinner parties *this* decade. You can make it days ahead (it gets better with time) and have it sitting in the refrigerator for the moment your guests have finished their dinners and started to look like they're getting snacky all over again. Then you emerge, like a hero, from the kitchen with a dish of cocoa-dusted, nostalgia-and-brandy-soaked tiramisu.

½ cup plus 2 tablespoons sugar

¼ cup plus 2 tablespoons brandy

2 tablespoons instant espresso powder

1½ cups boiling water

4 large egg yolks

Pinch of table salt

1 pound mascarpone cheese, softened

1 teaspoon vanilla paste (or 1 tablespoon pure vanilla extract)

½ teaspoon finely grated orange zest (optional)

1½ cups heavy cream

36 large Savoiardi cookies (ladyfingers), from 2 (7-ounce) packages

4 ounces bittersweet chocolate, very finely chopped

2 tablespoons unsweetened cocoa

1. In a medium heat-proof bowl, combine 2 tablespoons of the sugar, 2 tablespoons of the brandy, the espresso powder, and the boiling water, stirring to dissolve the sugar. Let cool.

2. In a medium bowl, combine the egg yolks, salt, the remaining ¼ cup of brandy, and the remaining ½ cup of sugar and whisk until smooth. Set the bowl over a pot filled with 1 inch of just-simmering water. Cook, whisking constantly, until the sugar is dissolved and the mixture is thick, pale, and doubled in volume, about 8 minutes. Remove the bowl from the pot and gently whisk in the mascarpone, vanilla paste, and orange zest, if using.

3. In a separate bowl, beat the heavy cream until soft peaks form. Scrape the whipped cream into the mascarpone mixture and, using a rubber spatula, gently fold together.

4. Working with 1 ladyfinger at a time, dip the whole cookie very briefly into the espresso mixture and arrange it in an 8 x 11-inch (2-quart) glass or ceramic baking dish. To avoid sogginess, be careful not to oversaturate the ladyfingers. Repeat, using half of the ladyfingers to cover the bottom of the baking dish in neat rows. Spoon half of the mascarpone mixture over the ladyfingers and sprinkle with the chopped chocolate. Repeat with the remaining ladyfingers, espresso mixture (you'll have some left over; don't be tempted to pour it over the ladyfingers), and mascarpone mixture, spreading it to the edges of the dish. Lightly dust the surface with cocoa. Cover and refrigerate until firm, at least 6 hours, preferably overnight, before serving.

BUTTERSCOTCH BUDINO
with SALTED CARAMEL SAUCE

In the 1980s and '90s, *budino* took Italian restaurants in the United States by storm. The pudding, often flavored with caramel or butterscotch, was a quick, inexpensive dessert for kitchen staffs to make that didn't involve any cooking on the fly or fussy plating. These same qualities make it a great party trick. You can make it the day before you have people over, pour it into ramekins, jars, mismatched champagne coupes, chipped teacups–whatever you have enough of in your cupboard. Then, when it's time to eat, give each one a drizzle of warm, salty caramel sauce and a spoonful of whipped cream.

Budino

2¾ cups whole milk

1½ cups heavy cream

1 cup dark brown sugar

1 teaspoon coarse
kosher salt (preferably
Diamond Crystal)

1 large egg plus 3 large
egg yolks

¼ cup plus 2 tablespoons
cornstarch

2 tablespoons unsalted
butter

1 tablespoon Scotch
or dark rum

Sweetened whipped cream,
for serving

Flaky sea salt (like Maldon
or Jacobsen), for serving

Caramel Sauce

½ cup granulated sugar

2 tablespoons light corn
syrup

½ cup heavy cream

1 teaspoon vanilla paste
(or ¼ vanilla bean, seeds
scraped)

2 tablespoons unsalted
butter

1. **Make the budino:** Set a fine-mesh sieve over a heat-proof bowl and place it near the stove. In a measuring cup, combine the heavy cream and milk. In a 3- to 4-quart heavy-bottomed saucepan, combine the brown sugar, ½ cup water, and the salt and bring to a boil. Cook over medium-high heat, without stirring, until the sugar is deep brown and reduced to a thin syrup (like maple syrup), 7 to 8 minutes. Immediately whisk in the milk and cream mixture and bring to a simmer. Remove the butterscotch from the heat.

2. In a medium bowl, whisk the whole egg, egg yolks, and cornstarch. Slowly add 1 cup of the warm butterscotch to the bowl, whisking constantly. Continuing to whisk constantly, return the egg–butterscotch mixture to the saucepan and bring to a simmer. Cook over moderately low heat, whisking constantly, until the custard is very thick, about 2 minutes. Remove from the heat and whisk in the butter and Scotch. Immediately pour the custard through the sieve into the bowl and press to remove any lumps. Carefully pour the mixture into 8 ramekins or half-pint jars. Cover and refrigerate until completely chilled, at least 4 hours or up to 2 days.

3. **Make the caramel sauce:** In a 2- to 3-quart saucepan, combine the granulated sugar, corn syrup, and 2 tablespoons water. Cook over medium-high heat without stirring, but gently swirling the pan occasionally, until the caramel is a medium amber color (like maple syrup), about 5 minutes. Remove the saucepan from the heat and, using a long-handled whisk, carefully add the cream, vanilla paste, and butter (the caramel will vigorously bubble as the cream is added). Pour into a heat-proof pitcher and let cool slightly.

4. **Serve the budino:** Serve each *budino* topped with the warm caramel sauce, whipped cream, and a pinch of flaky sea salt.

NUTELLASAGNA

When chef and writer Allison Robicelli introduced Nutellasagna to the menu at her Brooklyn bakery, Robicelli's, she meant it as a cheeky response to the absurd stunt dishes that restaurants had started concocting in the hope they would go viral–the rainbow-hued, gold-encrusted monstrosities of the world. She never expected what happened next. People went crazy for the sweet, hazelnutty, marshmallow-topped lasagna. Fans wrote about it, Instagrammed it, and lined up down the block for a taste. Now that Robicelli's is closed, Allison has retired the dish, but we decided to immortalize the recipe in this book. If you have trouble tracking down gelatin, or just don't want to make your own marshmallow topping, you can skip steps 7 through 10 and pour a bag of mini marshmallows over the top before broiling.

Nutellasagna

1 pound mascarpone cheese

15 ounces ricotta cheese

1¼ cups confectioners' sugar

¼ cup whole milk or half-and-half

1 tablespoon cornstarch

2 large eggs

1 tablespoon vanilla extract

8 ounces chopped skinned hazelnuts (2 cups)

8 tablespoons (1 stick) unsalted butter plus ½ tablespoon melted unsalted butter

Coarse kosher salt (preferably Diamond Crystal)

Zest of 1 large orange

18 to 20 no-boil lasagna noodles (from about 2 boxes; see Note at left)

1½ cups Nutella (from two 7.7-ounce jars)

1½ cups heavy cream

NOTE
If using dried, curly noodles, arrange 15 precooked noodles in 3 layers and bake uncovered the entire time.

Marshmallow Topping

½ cup plus 3 tablespoons granulated sugar

¼ cup corn syrup

2 pinches of cream of tartar

4 large egg whites

½ packet (1¼ teaspoons or ⅛ ounce) gelatin

¼ teaspoon coarse kosher salt (preferably Diamond crystal)

½ teaspoon vanilla extract

½ teaspoon hazelnut extract (optional)

(recipe continues)

1. *Make the mascarpone filling:*
Preheat the oven to 350°F and position a rack in the center. Using a mixer, beat together the mascarpone, ricotta, confectioners' sugar, milk, and cornstarch until smooth, then beat in the eggs and the vanilla. Set aside.

2. *Toast the hazelnuts:* Place the hazelnuts on a rimmed baking sheet lined with parchment paper and toast in the oven until fragrant, about 5 minutes. Immediately toss with the ½ tablespoon of melted butter and a pinch of salt; set aside to cool.

3. *Make the orange butter:* Cook the remaining 8 tablespoons of butter in a medium saucepan over medium-low heat until the milk solids turn a medium shade of amber and the butter begins to smell nutty, about 2 minutes. Remove from the heat; add the orange zest and stir well. Cover to keep warm.

4. *Prepare the noodles:* Fill a large baking pan or pasta pot with hot water. Add the noodles one at a time to prevent sticking. Allow to sit for 5 minutes until softened; drain. Place several 2-foot-long pieces of parchment paper on your counter. Using a paper towel, pat any excess water off each noodle, then lay them on the parchment. Lightly brush the tops with some of the orange butter.

5. Scoop the Nutella into a large heat-proof bowl. Heat the cream to a near boil, then pour over the Nutella while whisking vigorously.

6. *Assemble the Nutellasagna:* Brush a 9 x 13-inch (3-quart) glass or ceramic baking dish with orange butter, making sure the bottom of the pan is well coated. Place about 4 or 5 noodles in the dish in an even layer, then pour on a thick layer of mascarpone cream, spreading with a spatula to even out. Next, grab the Nutella sauce and generously drizzle across the mascarpone cream layer, then sprinkle with one third of the chopped hazelnuts. Repeat for 3 more layers, ending with a thin layer of mascarpone cream on top. Cover tightly with aluminum foil and bake for 45 minutes to an hour, until the top layer looks puffy. (Start the marshmallow topping while the Nutellasagna bakes.)

7. *Make the marshmallow topping:*
In a heavy-bottomed saucepan affixed with a digital or candy thermometer, combine ½ cup water with ½ cup of the granulated sugar, the corn syrup, and a pinch of cream of tartar. Cook over high heat to the soft boil stage (235°F).

8. In the meantime, using a mixer, beat the egg whites on high speed with another pinch of cream of tartar until soft peaks form. Add the remaining 3 tablespoons granulated sugar and continue beating on high speed until medium peaks form, then turn off the mixer. Add ¼ cup water to a measuring cup, sprinkle the gelatin over the top to soften; set aside.

9. When the sugar reaches the soft boil stage, turn the mixer back on to medium speed. Carefully drizzle the hot sugar syrup down the side of the bowl, going very slowly so that you don't scramble the eggs. The marshmallow will gain significant volume during this step. Once all the sugar is added, turn off the mixer, add the gelatin and the salt, then turn the mixer back on to medium-high speed. Beat until the bottom of the bowl is cool to the touch, 10 to 15 minutes. Add the vanilla and the hazelnut extract, if using, and beat for an additional minute to incorporate.

10. Top and finish the Nutellasagna: Raise the oven rack up to the upper-middle position, then preheat the broiler to high. Using an offset spatula, cover the Nutellasagna with peaks of marshmallow. Place under the broiler until brown and toasty, 5 to 10 minutes, depending on your personal tastes and the intensity of your oven. If desired, cover the top with additional Nutella cream and toasted hazelnuts before serving.

NOTE

Nutellasagna can be served hot, at room temperature, or cold. If serving hot, make the marshmallow topping while the Nutellasagna is baking, and allow the Nutellasagna to rest for 15 minutes before proceeding. Otherwise, wrap the Nutellasagna well and place in the refrigerator or freezer until the day you're intending to serve, as the marshmallow tastes best when it's made the day of.

THE BUILDING BLOCKS

As much as we like to think that lasagna is greater than the sum of its parts, each of those parts should taste as good as possible before it makes its way into the baking dish. Sometimes it's just a matter of making a perfectly chewy, slightly eggy pasta dough. Sometimes it's tasting your ricotta and adding a few cranks of pepper before spooning it across a layer of pasta. And sometimes it's getting the béchamel to just the perfect thickness so that it stays creamy while it bakes without making the pasta too soggy.

This chapter will get you started on the right foot with fresh pasta, flavored ricottas, meaty ragus, and a tomato sauce that you'll find yourself using again and again in baked zitis, improvisational lasagnas, and as a makeshift dipping sauce for garlic knots.

ANNA®
NAPOLETANA
14.99
100% Italian
FARINA DI GRANO TENERO
TIPO "00"
EXTRA FINE FLOUR

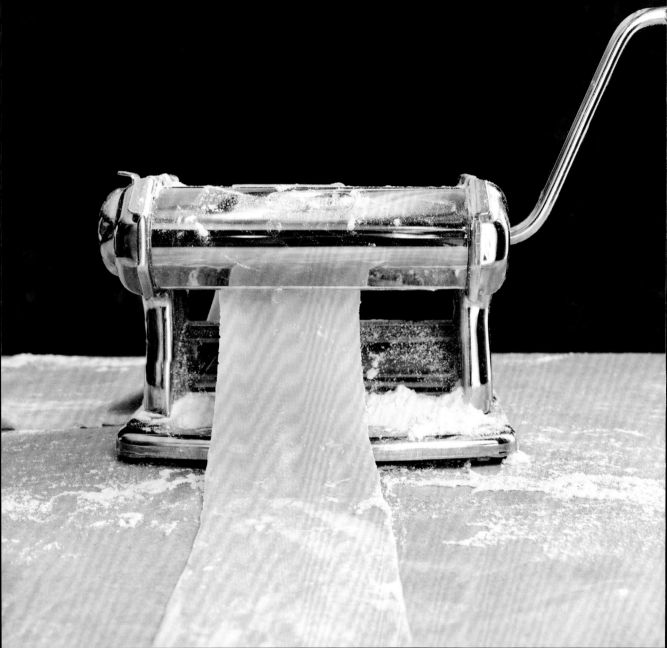

FRESH PASTA SHEETS

Making fresh pasta from scratch will change how you think about lasagna. Your noodles will be thinner and more delicate than the dried kind, soaking up the flavor of the sauce without becoming gummy or slippery, and retaining a satisfying eggy chew.

MAKES
1 POUND
OF DOUGH
(12 SHEETS;
ENOUGH FOR
1 LARGE
LASAGNA OR
2 SMALLER
ONES)

2 cups all-purpose flour (9½ ounces), plus more for rolling

3 large eggs, at room temperature

1 tablespoon extra-virgin olive oil

1 teaspoon coarse kosher salt (preferably Diamond Crystal), plus more for boiling

1. Place the flour, eggs, olive oil, and salt in a food processor and pulse in 1-second intervals until the dough is moistened and comes together in small beads that resemble couscous. Don't let the dough form a ball.

2. Turn the dough out onto a work surface and knead (without adding flour) until smooth and elastic, 2 to 3 minutes (the dough will be almost too stiff to knead). Wrap the dough in plastic and set aside at room temperature to rest for 30 minutes or up to an hour (the dough will soften and be easy to work with after sitting).

3. Arrange several clean kitchen towels on a work surface and dust them lightly with flour. Cut the dough into quarters and cover 3 pieces with a damp towel. Flatten 1 piece of the dough and dust it lightly with flour. Roll the dough through a pasta machine, starting on the lowest (widest) setting. Fold the rolled dough into thirds like a letter, then roll it through again, feeding the open, less wide end (the side where you can see the fold) through the machine first. Repeat three times, then start to roll the dough using thinner settings,

folding it and putting it through the same setting two times before progressing to the next thinner setting, and flouring the dough as needed to keep it from sticking. Work your way through to the second to last setting (#6 on most machines, or the thickness of two playing cards). The completely rolled sheet should measure 4 to 5 inches wide and 22 to 24 inches long.

4. Cut into three 8-inch sheets and place them on the floured kitchen towels. Repeat with the other 3 pieces of dough. Turn the sheets on the kitchen towels occasionally so they dry slightly. They should be pliable but a bit leathery.

5. Bring a large pot of salted water to a boil. Boil the pasta in 2 batches, cooking just until the pasta is tender and the color changes from deep yellow to pale yellow, about 1 minute. Remove the sheets, drain, and rinse briefly with cold water. Arrange the lasagna sheets on clean kitchen towels, pressing them slightly to flatten. Use immediately or keep covered at room temperature for up to an hour.

CLASSIC **&** SIMPLE RED SAUCE

Having a few jars of red sauce in the refrigerator or freezer is like having the security of a little extra money saved away in the bank. Not only does this incredibly versatile ingredient come in handy when you're facing a dinner-related emergency, but it also whittles away your prep time when making a more involved baked pasta or lasagna. This sauce is simple, vegetarian, and adaptable–and the focus is on the flavor of the canned tomatoes themselves. So whether you're throwing together a Baked Ziti (page 89) or constructing an Eggplant Parm Lasagna (page 53), this is the sauce that will have your back.

1 (28-ounce) can whole peeled tomatoes

2 tablespoons extra-virgin olive oil

1 small yellow onion, finely chopped

2 large garlic cloves, minced

4 tablespoons tomato paste

2 teaspoons sugar

½ teaspoon dried oregano, crumbled

1 dried bay leaf

Coarse kosher salt (preferably Diamond Crystal) and freshly ground black pepper

1. Using kitchen shears, cut the tomatoes in the can until finely chopped. Heat the olive oil in a large saucepan over medium-high heat until shimmering, about 2 minutes.

2. Add the onion and garlic and cook, stirring occasionally, until lightly browned, about 5 minutes. Add the tomato paste and cook, stirring gently, until the paste darkens slightly, 1 to 2 minutes.

3. Add the canned tomatoes and their juices, the sugar, oregano, bay leaf, and 2 cups water. Break up any large pieces of tomato with a spoon. Season with 1 teaspoon salt and a pinch of pepper and bring to a boil.

1. Cover the saucepan partially, reduce the heat to medium-low, and simmer until the sauce is thick and reduced to about 4½ cups, 35 to 40 minutes. Season to taste with salt and pepper. Discard the bay leaf. The sauce can be refrigerated in an airtight container for up to 4 days, or frozen for up to 3 months.

RAGU BOLOGNESE

MAKES
6 CUPS
(ENOUGH FOR
1 LASAGNA
PLUS
LEFTOVERS)

The ideal Bolognese, which takes its name from the northern Italian city of Bologna, combines the smoke and salt of cured pork (sometimes bacon, but in this case pancetta) with rich ground pork and beef. As the mix simmers in a combination of chicken broth and milk, the liquid reduces, and the whole thing is condensed into a buttery, aromatic sauce. Since the sauce gets better after a day or two in the fridge, we highly recommend making a double batch so you can have some for bucatini tonight and plenty to turn into lasagna next week.

4 tablespoons (½ stick) unsalted butter

¼ cup extra-virgin olive oil

1 large yellow onion, cut into ¼-inch dice (1½ cups)

1 large carrot, cut into ¼-inch dice (¾ cup)

2 celery ribs, cut into ¼-inch dice (¾ cup)

2 large garlic cloves, minced

4 ounces pancetta, cut into ¼-inch dice

1 pound ground beef (85% lean)

1 pound ground pork

Coarse kosher salt (preferably Diamond Crystal) and freshly ground black pepper

1 (6-ounce) can tomato paste

2 cups whole milk, warm

2 dried bay leaves

6 fresh thyme sprigs

1 cup semidry white wine, such as white Burgundy or Sauvignon Blanc

2 cups low-sodium chicken broth

1. In a large heavy-bottomed pot, melt the butter with the olive oil over medium heat. Add the onion, carrot, and celery and cook, stirring occasionally, until softened but not browned, 5 to 6 minutes. Stir in the garlic and cook until fragrant, about 1 minute.

2. Add the pancetta, beef, and pork and stir to break the meat into small bits. Add 1 teaspoon salt and ¼ teaspoon pepper. Increase the heat to medium-high and cook, stirring frequently, until the liquid is completely evaporated and the meat is beginning to brown, about 15 minutes. Be sure to stir and scrape up any bits from the bottom of the pan with a wooden spoon to avoid scorching.

3. Add the tomato paste and cook, stirring, until it darkens slightly, 1 to 2 minutes. Add the warm milk, bay leaves, and thyme and cook, scraping up the browned bits from the bottom of the pan, until the milk is reduced by half, about 5 minutes. Stir in the wine and simmer over medium-low heat, stirring occasionally, until nearly reduced and the smell of alcohol dissipates, about 10 minutes.

4. Stir in the chicken broth and simmer over medium-low heat, uncovered, stirring occasionally, until the ragu is richly flavored and reduced to 6 cups, about 30 minutes longer. Season with salt and pepper and discard the bay leaves and thyme sprigs. The sauce can be refrigerated in an airtight container for up to 4 days, or frozen for up to 3 months.

SUNDAY SAUCE

MAKES
8 CUPS OF
STRAINED
SAUCE,
PLUS 24
MEATBALLS
AND
2 POUNDS
OF PORK
(ENOUGH FOR
2 LASAGNAS)

The secrets to an unforgettable Sunday gravy are meat and time. This one brings together three different meats with totally different flavors and textures: Italian sausage full of fennel seeds and red pepper flakes, springy beef meatballs packed with thyme and Parmesan, and a meaty pork shoulder that pulls apart as it cooks down into the sauce. The ideal way to cook this is on a relaxed afternoon while reading the Sunday *New York Times* (or your Twitter feed) between stirs, with some Pavarotti arias (or *Drums and Wires*) wafting in from a speaker in another room.

Tomato Sauce

¼ cup extra-virgin olive oil

2 pounds boneless pork shoulder, cut into 1½-inch cubes

2 teaspoons coarse kosher salt (preferably Diamond Crystal)

½ teaspoon freshly ground black pepper

1 pound sweet or hot Italian sausage links or a combination

1 large yellow onion, finely chopped (1½ cups)

4 large garlic cloves, minced (1½ tablespoons)

1 (6-ounce) can tomato paste

2 (28-ounce) cans peeled Italian tomatoes, coarsely chopped in their cans

1 (28-ounce) can tomato puree

2 tablespoons sugar

3 dried bay leaves

1½ teaspoons dried oregano

Meatballs

1 teaspoon extra-virgin olive oil

1 medium yellow onion, minced (1 cup)

1 large garlic clove, minced

1 teaspoon dried thyme

½ teaspoon dried rosemary, crushed

¼ cup whole milk

3 slices firm white sandwich bread, torn

1 large egg, beaten

2 tablespoons freshly grated Parmesan cheese

2 tablespoons finely chopped fresh flat-leaf Italian parsley

2 teaspoons coarse kosher salt (preferably Diamond Crystal)

½ teaspoon freshly ground black pepper

1½ pounds ground beef, 85% lean (or ¾ lbs each beef and pork)

Vegetable oil, for frying

All-purpose flour, for dusting

1. Make the tomato sauce: Heat the oil in a large heavy pot or Dutch oven over medium-high heat until shimmering, about 2 minutes. Season the pork with 1 teaspoon of the salt and ¼ teaspoon of the pepper and cook it in batches, turning occasionally, until browned all over, 8 to 10 minutes per batch. Use a slotted spoon to transfer the meat to a platter as it browns. Prick the sausages with a fork and then add them to the pot and cook, turning occasionally, until browned but not cooked through, about 8 minutes. Transfer the sausages to the platter and refrigerate until you are ready to use them.

2. Add the onion and garlic to the pot and cook, stirring, until translucent, 3 to 4 minutes. Add the tomato paste and cook, stirring, until it darkens slightly, 1 to 2 minutes. Return the browned pork shoulder to the pot. Add the canned tomatoes, tomato puree, sugar, bay leaves, oregano, and 4 cups water. Season with the remaining teaspoon of salt and ¼ teaspoon of pepper and bring to a boil. Reduce the heat to low and cook, partially covered, stirring to the bottom of the pot occasionally, until the meat is tender and the sauce is slightly thickened, about 1½ hours.

3. Meanwhile, make the meatballs: Heat the oil in a large skillet over medium-high heat until shimmering, about 2 minutes. Add the onion, garlic, thyme, and rosemary and cook until translucent, 3 to 4 minutes. Transfer to a large bowl and let cool, then add the milk and bread and let soak until moistened. Add the egg, Parmesan, parsley, salt, and pepper and knead until combined. Add the ground beef and knead until evenly mixed. Divide the meat into 24 portions and roll into balls. Rinse and dry the skillet.

1. Once the sauce has cooked for 1½ hours, heat ½ inch of vegetable oil in a large skillet over medium heat until shimmering, about 2 minutes. Dust the meatballs with flour, tapping off the excess, and add half of them to the skillet. Cook over medium-high heat, turning occasionally, until the meatballs are browned all over but not cooked through, about 3 minutes. Using a slotted spoon, add the meatballs to the sauce as they brown and repeat with the remaining meatballs. Cut the browned sausages into ½-inch-thick rounds and add to the sauce along with the meatballs. Simmer, uncovered, until the meatballs and sausages are cooked through, about 30 minutes.

5. Discard the bay leaves and use the sauce immediately, refrigerate it in an airtight container for up to 4 days, or freeze for up to 3 months.

7 FLAVORED RICOTTAS

If béchamel is the calling card of a northern Italian–style lasagna, then ricotta cheese is definitely the key ingredient to lasagnas with origins in the south of Italy (any Napoletana-style lasagnas, for instance). A great counterpunch to melty, stretchy cheeses like mozzarella or Fontina, ricotta tends to hold its creaminess at most temperatures and is also a convenient vessel for flavor and color. While many lasagna recipes call for straight-up ricotta, it's fun to enrich the ricotta with mix-ins for an extra layer of flavor. Here are some of our favorite combinations to experiment with and sub in as you go.

For 2 pounds of ricotta, add the following mix-ins before adding eggs (all can be halved for 1 pound of ricotta).

Pesto Swirled Ricotta

¼ cup freshly grated Pecorino Romano cheese mixed with ricotta, 2 teaspoons coarse kosher salt, ½ teaspoon freshly ground black pepper, and ¼ cup fresh pesto gently swirled in.

Mixed–Herb Ricotta

2 tablespoons chopped fresh flat-leaf parsley, 2 tablespoons chopped fresh chives, 1 teaspoon chopped fresh rosemary, 1 teaspoon chopped fresh thyme, 2 teaspoons coarse kosher salt, and ½ teaspoon freshly ground black pepper

Porcini Ricotta

½ cup dried porcini mushrooms soaked in boiling water for 15 minutes, then drained and finely chopped, then sautéed in extra-virgin olive oil with ½ cup chopped shallots (about 1 large shallot); 1 teaspoon chopped fresh thyme; 2 teaspoons coarse kosher salt; and ½ teaspoon freshly ground black pepper

Greens & Ricotta

1 cup cooked (and pressed) greens, such as spinach, kale, mustard greens, and chard, sautéed with 1 tablespoon chopped garlic and ¼ teaspoon dried red pepper flakes; 2 teaspoons coarse kosher salt; and ½ teaspoon freshly ground black pepper

Roasted Garlic–Parmesan Ricotta

1 head of garlic, roasted and mashed (see page 95); ¼ cup freshly grated Parmesan cheese, 2 teaspoons coarse kosher salt, and ½ teaspoon freshly ground black pepper

Carrot–Parsley Ricotta

1 cup coarsely grated carrots sautéed with ½ cup chopped onion, ¼ cup chopped fresh flat-leaf parsley, 2 teaspoons coarse kosher salt, and ½ teaspoon freshly ground black pepper

Roasted Poblano Pepper (or Chile) Ricotta

¾ cup chopped roasted peppers and ¼ cup freshly grated Pecorino Romano cheese (or poblanos and grated cotija cheese), 2 teaspoons coarse kosher salt, and ½ teaspoon freshly ground black pepper

CRESPELLE

Like béchamel sauce, legend has it that crepes made their way into French cuisine with the help of Catherine de' Medici, who took the delicate, round pancakes with her to Paris from Florence when she became the queen of France at the age of fourteen. The spongy, tender crepes can be layered with fillings, like a lasagna, or wrapped into little cylinders around a flavored ricotta and covered in sauce, like a manicotti. When they're rolled up into a cigar and thinly sliced crosswise, they can even turn into long, flat noodle-like ribbons called *scripelle* to soak up a sauce or a broth.

MAKES
ABOUT
20 (6-INCH)
CRESPELLE
(ENOUGH FOR
SWEET
CRESPELLE
WITH LEMON
& TART
CHERRY
SAUCE, PAGE
116) OR
SPINACH
MANICOTTI
WITH
CREAMY
TOMATO
SAUCE, PAGE
95)

1 cup plus 2 tablespoons all-purpose flour (5 ounces)

4 large eggs

1¾ cups whole milk

3 tablespoons extra-virgin olive oil or grapeseed oil (see Note), plus more for the pan

½ teaspoon coarse kosher salt (preferably Diamond Crystal)

1. Combine the flour, eggs, milk, oil, and salt in a blender and mix on medium-low speed until smooth. Set aside at room temperature to rest for 20 minutes (the batter will thicken slightly as it sits).

2. Brush a 6- or 7-inch nonstick skillet or crepe pan lightly with oil and set over medium-high heat. Spoon 2½ to 3 tablespoons of the batter into the hot pan and quickly tilt and swirl the skillet to evenly coat the bottom and a bit up the sides of the pan with batter. Cook until the *crespella* is brown around the edges and the center is just set, about 30 seconds.

3. Loosen the *crespella* from the pan with the tip of a knife, then using your fingers or a spatula, flip and cook just until set and lightly golden, about 10 seconds longer. Transfer the *crespella* to a plate. Repeat, brushing the skillet with oil between batches and reducing the heat as needed if the batter sputters in the skillet or the *crespelle* brown too quickly. Stack the *crespelle* as they are finished and cool completely before using. To make ahead, wrap the stack tightly in plastic wrap and refrigerate for up to 2 days.

NOTE

To make sweet crespelle *for Sweet Crespelle with Lemon & Tart Cherry Sauce on page 116 or Sweet Crespelle Lasagna on page 117, substitute 3 tablespoons melted unsalted butter for the oil and add 1 tablespoon sugar.*

CLASSIC BÉCHAMEL

This is the best recipe for béchamel you will ever find written in a book. It really is. Béchamel is one of France's mother sauces, but believe it or not, it originated in Tuscany and dates back to the Renaissance. It's made by whisking milk into a roux (a combination of flour and butter) until the whole mixture becomes a thick, creamy vessel for flavor. Typically, it's flavored with a tiny, barely noticeable pinch of nutmeg, but you can also melt a little Parmesan into it (which, to some, might technically ease it into Mornay territory–a béchamel sauce with cheese). Béchamel is the key ingredient for making mac and cheese that won't congeal into a giant brick the second it comes out of the oven and is also a foundational ingredient in many lasagnas, creating the perfect barrier between layers of pasta and layers of meat sauce or vegetables. When you're looking for a thicker, fluffier béchamel with a little more structure, use the variation below.

4 tablespoons (½ stick) unsalted butter

¼ cup all-purpose flour

4 cups (1 quart) whole milk

1 teaspoon coarse kosher salt (preferably Diamond Crystal)

¼ teaspoon freshly ground white pepper

Pinch of freshly grated nutmeg

1. In a large saucepan set over medium heat, melt the butter. Add the flour and cook, whisking constantly, until pale golden, 3 to 4 minutes.

2. Add the milk all at once, whisking constantly, and bring to a boil. Reduce the heat to very low and cook, whisking, until the sauce is thickened, about 5 minutes. Season with the salt, white pepper, and nutmeg. If not using the sauce immediately, transfer it to a bowl and cover with plastic wrap, pressing directly onto the surface of the sauce to prevent a skin from forming; refrigerate for up to 2 days.

~~~~~~~~~~~~~~~~~~~~~~~~~~~~~

VARIATION
Thick Béchamel

To make a thick béchamel, follow this recipe using 8 tablespoons (1 stick) unsalted butter and ½ cup all-purpose flour.

ACKNOWLEDGMENTS

How much lasagna can one person eat in six months? A lot, it turns out. But we couldn't have come close to finishing this book without all of the people who pitched in ideas, recipes, and advice along the way, or without the people who bravely lent their stomachs to the cause throughout a long year of baked pasta experimentation.

So much of the heart and soul of this book comes from the recipes of Grace Parisi, who spent hours chatting over coffee and spitballing crazy ideas over the phone with me, evolving them into even better ideas in her kitchen. Grace is the genius who taught us that if you have a skillet, some frozen ravioli, and half an hour, you can turn it into lasagna.

We were also lucky enough to publish guest recipes from a few contributors and friends of *TASTE*, including Mark Ladner, Michael Solomonov, Hannah Giorgis, Cathy Erway, and Allison Robicelli.

Thanks to the keen-eyed photographer duo Dylan James Ho + Jeni Afuso, who kept the photo studio alight with good humor and plenty of Frank Ocean. Thanks to Vivian Lui, who cooked and styled all of the food that made it into the photos in this book (cheese pulls and all), and to Nidia Cueva and PropLink for setting us up with all of the enamel pans, checked tablecloths, and grandmotherly dishes of our dreams.

In addition to the photos we shot at PropLink, Dylan and Jeni and I spent a sunny October afternoon in a few of Los Angeles's most old-school Italian institutions. Dolce Vita, Casa Bianca, and Roma Market were incredibly welcoming to us, and Rosario from Roma Market kept us well-fed with his famous pink paper-wrapped sandwiches. (If you're ever in Pasadena with a bit of real estate in your stomach, "The Sandwich" is non-negotiable.)

Thanks to Raquel Pelzel, our fearless editor at Clarkson Potter, who infused an incredible amount of her own creativity, energy, and home cooking wisdom into this book. Thanks to Jen Wang, Stephanie Huntwork, and Marysarah Quinn for their discerning art direction and patience when we asked questions like, "Can we make this font more lasagna-y?" Thanks to David Hawk, Allison Renzulli, Windy Dorresteyn, and the publicity and marketing team at Clarkson Potter for helping us tell the world about this book.

Thanks to Lorena Jones, Doris Cooper, Aaron Wehner, and Talia Baiocchi for all of the support they've given the *TASTE* team (Matt Rodbard, Tatiana Bautista, and me) as this book came together.

—Anna Hezel and the editors of TASTE

INDEX

Copyright © 2019
by The Editors of *TASTE*

Photography copyright © 2019
by Dylan James Ho + Jeni Afuso

All rights reserved.
Published in the United States by
Clarkson Potter/Publishers,
an imprint of Random House, a
division of Penguin Random
House LLC, New York.
clarksonpotter.com

CLARKSON POTTER is a trademark
and POTTER with colophon is a
registered trademark of Penguin
Random House LLC.

Library of Congress Cataloging-in-
Publication Data
Title: Lasagna : a baked pasta
cookbook / the Editors of Taste.
Description: First edition. | New York:
Clarkson Potter/Publishers, 2019.
Identifiers: LCCN 2018049004| ISBN
9781984824066 | ISBN
9781984824073 (ebook)
Subjects: LCSH: Cooking, Italian. |
Cooking (Pasta) | LCGFT: Cookbooks.
Classification: LCC TX809.M17 L358
2019 | DDC 641.5945–dc23 LC
record available at
https://lccn.loc.gov/2018049004

ISBN 978-1-9848-2406-6
Ebook ISBN 978-1-9848-2407-3

Printed in China

Book and cover design by Jen Wang
Cover photographs:
Dylan James Ho + Jeni Afuso

10 9 8 7 6 5 4 3 2 1

First Edition